10 STEPS TO PUBLISH & SUCCEED

How to Put Your Best Book Forward

JILL RONSLEY

BLUE STAR PRESS INC

10 Steps to Publish and Succeed: How to Put Your Best Book Forward
by Jill Ronsley

ISBN: 978-0-9739952-1-3 (soft cover)
ISBN: 978-0-9739952-3-7 (e-book)

Printed and bound in the USA

10 9 8 7 6 5 4 3 2 1

Published by Blue Star Press Inc.
Vancouver, BC, Canada

Front cover design by Ian Stanbury
Interior design by Jill Ronsley
Author's photo by Ellen Reitman

For more information on writing, editing, design and book production, visit www.publishandsucceed.com and www.suneditwrite.com. Send an email to the author at jill@publishandsucceed.com or jill@suneditwrite.com.

To Joanne and Joe,
who gave me my first books, taught me to write
and filled my shelves with books of knowledge, literature and art

Contents

Display of softcover and hardcover books at a printing facility

The author reviewing finished products

How This Book
Can Help You with *Your* Book

FOR INDEPENDENT PUBLISHERS AND SMALL PRESSES, success depends on creating books with quality content that are well written, produced and distributed. Getting your book just right involves revisions and re-writes, time, passion and perseverance. Whether you are publishing print books or e-books, *10 Steps to Publish and Succeed: How to Put Your Best Book Forward* shares the secrets you need to know and reveals the mistakes you need to avoid to ensure you end up with a quality book that you are proud to put your name on and sell.

This book is a compilation of the insights I have gathered as a writer, editor, book designer, publisher and consultant over the past 15 years. While working with authors and publishers around the world, I have learned that many people have entertaining, interesting and valuable life experiences, which form the basis of good books—they just need help creating and marketing their publications while avoiding the pitfalls that frequently appear on the path.

Over the years, I have referred my clients to reputable illustrators, printers, booksellers and other industry professionals. With the benefit of these combined services, my clients have produced high-quality books that give them a great sense of satisfaction and offer their readers the chance to benefit from their creativity and knowledge. Many of these books have won awards, including the ForeWord Magazine Book Award, Benjamin Franklin Award, Eric Hoffer Award, Nautilus Book Award, Moonbeam Award, Next Generation Indie Book Award, Dan Poynter's Global Ebook Awards and others.

The motivation behind this book is to help those who are either publishing for the first time or branching out into new areas of publishing and book marketing, and for that reason, I have included both well-established and new information about this ever-changing field. *10 Steps to Publish and Succeed* is a resource for anyone who wants to produce a well-edited, well-designed book; who needs to know about e-book creation; who wants to ensure his photos and illustrations are effective; and who needs a wide range of online and offline marketing ideas to help him succeed.

Clearly organized for at-a-glance referencing, the information, resources and anecdotes I have included will show you not only *how*, but also *why* this book can help you put your own best book forward. With your book published, it *can* stand out from the competition and succeed!

How can you publish your best book?

With the continuous advance of small press publishing, independent (self) publishing and e-publishing, more books are produced now than ever before. New media forms have breathed fresh life into the publishing industry, with the Internet providing a vast and fertile ground for creative marketing. The opportunities for book production, promotion, marketing and reading keep multiplying, so it is much easier to produce and succeed with your book today than it would have been five years ago, or even two years ago. Of course, with publishing so much more accessible, you face more competition, too, so, you have to develop your skills to make your mark. Your book *must* stand out!

While reading and technology may seem incongruous, electronic devices, such as tablets and smart phones, have given everyone—and notably young people—a renewed interest in reading. This is partly because this generation's love affair with the new media has created a vibrant, creative culture that wants to learn and express. The digital age, combined with innate human curiosity, the desire to learn and the urge to create, has renewed people's interest in all forms of publishing—including the printed book.

Publishing is skyrocketing. In fact, studies show that 57 percent of adults read at least one paperback in 2012, and 22 percent read an e-book—an increase of three percent and five percent, respectively, from 2011.[1] What does this mean for you? With more people reading, you have a better opportunity to have your book published and see it succeed than ever before. However, your success is dependent on many factors, so whether your book is nonfiction or fiction, and regardless of your subject or genre, grasping the elements of publishing is essential if you are to take full advantage the new opportunities.

Whether you have written your book or you are still writing it, you know it contains valuable information or is a great story. All you need to do now is produce it well so others can benefit from it and enjoy it.

To publish ... or to publish independently? That is the question!

Choosing the right publishing route is not easy, and for many authors, deciding between traditional publishing and independent publishing is the most trying dilemma they face. This book can empower you with the knowledge needed to choose what is best for you and your book.

If you plan to submit your manuscript to a traditional publishing house, your book has to be well written and interesting, no doubt, but also well edited and proofread. The publisher will take care of the book design, cover design, cost of production and basic promotion. If the book is for children, the publisher will choose an illustrator. In fact, the author has restricted input into the publishing process and receives very little information about it. In recent years, traditional publishers have been taking less responsibility for marketing, leaving much of that burden on the author. An author's ability to promote his book actively is often influential when a publisher is deciding whether to accept a submission or reject it. Increasingly, clauses requiring the author to market his book are written into contracts. However, knowledge is power, and the more you know about the publishing process, the more control you have over your book. If it is accepted by more than one publisher, a thorough understanding of book production will help you make informed choices and negotiate clauses in your contract so they are in your favor.

- *10 Steps to Publish and Succeed* will not only help you understand publishing in general—it will inform you in detail about the vast potential of independent publishing. Following its 10 well-defined steps will help you avoid unnecessary expense and frustration and achieve success.
- If your book does well, you stand to gain a greater profit from independent publishing than traditional publishing. If it doesn't sell, you will lose more because your investment will have been greater. If it sustains best-seller status for more than a week or two, bravo! Either avenue will serve you well.

Independent publishing (self-publishing)

In this book, I have used the term "independent publishing" instead of "self-publishing" in most instances. I feel that "independent" better describes the work of the publisher who produces his or her own books in any genre. Publishing is publishing. It involves editing a written text, designing the book for print and electronic production, marketing and distribution.

The word "self-publishing" is an anachronism that has developed moot connotations for serious publishers and readers today. In particular, it is associated with vanity publishing and poor quality. But many independently produced books have excellent quality, from content and writing to design and printing. Some have sustained the status of bestseller. The aim of this book is to ensure that independent publishers can achieve the highest standard of production and succeed in their endeavors.

I believe that just as the film industry respects the originality and value of well-made independent films and considers them an important category in the arts, so the publishing industry should do the same with independent books, and will steadily move in that direction. Quality must be acknowledged and respected wherever it is. The reading public and unbiased reviewers have the ability and power to decide what is good, interesting and worthwhile, whether a book is published traditionally or independently.

The growth of independent publishing

Traditional publishing still dominates the industry, and large publishing houses are adapting to the growth of e-publishing. But independent publishing is gaining recognition as a viable and sometimes preferable path. It offers more opportunities to both new and established writers as fresh resources and options evolve. It also offers the reading public more by lessening the power large publishing houses have to dictate what books are available. A mainstream publisher may have filled its quota in the memoir genre for the next two years, but an independent publisher is free to produce his memoir now, and readers can read it. Even if a topic is not hot, you can publish the book you are passionate about, and readers can read it.

Yes, poor-quality self-published books reach the marketplace, too—and that is the bane of self-publishing. But, as more independent publishers and small presses produce quality content in a professional manner, they strengthen the publishing industry as a whole. Despite the pros and cons of independent publishing, its growth is unstoppable.

According to an article by Gary Price published in October 2012, research conducted by Bowker, the official ISBN agency for the US and its territories, shows just how significant independent publishing has become. In 2011, almost 149,000 self-published print books constituted 43 percent of the total traditional print production for that year. Self-publishing contributed to the first substantial increase in print production from 2007 to 2011, which is particularly encouraging for small presses (publishers who have released 10 books or fewer) and self-publishers. Over that five-year period, print books grew 33 percent and e-book production was up 129 percent, while production by small presses increased more than 74 percent. CreateSpace's burgeoning growth (mostly non-traditional publishers) was an impressive 1,702 percent.[2]

There is no denying that the market is very competitive, but the good news is that it's a growing market and you have more opportunity than ever before to capitalize on that growth and succeed. You have to put your best book forward, and the 10 steps outlined in this book will give yours an advantage over the many flooding the market today.

The expansion of the publishing world through independent publishing, e-publishing, audio book publishing, the manufacture of e-reading tablets and devices, and the birth of new regional, global and online marketing techniques has invigorated people's interest in writing and reading. Those involved in the publishing industry—from writers to book producers to readers—have benefitted, creative opportunities have multiplied, and even the field of education is flourishing.

But for any publishing to succeed, the first essential ingredient is quality. As a small or independent publisher, you have to be sure that people are interested in your topic. Your book must be well written, without grammar, punctuation and spelling errors, which would only diminish its perceived value. Your book production must be professional, having a high standard of cover design, interior design and printing. And, of course, your book title must be marketable.

One of the main benefits of independent publishing is that most of the income from sales goes to the author (publisher), as opposed to the meager royalties earned through traditional publishing. However, it is almost impossible for one person to do everything at a professional level, so independent publishing does include expenses.

Some bestselling mainstream authors have turned to independent publishing to increase their revenues beyond what they could earn through traditional publishing. Of course, they already have an established platform, so quick self-publishing success is more likely for them than for new self-publishers.

Marketing is a key challenge new independent publishers face. People need to know about your book before they can buy it, and in order for them to know about it, you have to promote it diligently. Building a platform to become successful takes time and perseverance. Nick Morgan, a Forbes freelance contributor, describes a platform as "getting enough people to care about you and your book, through social media, traditional media, word of mouth, bake sales—any way you can. It's creating a community of people with a genuine interest in the idea you're putting forward. It's the way in which you create a strong brand around you and the book and get the world to pay attention."[3]

I know from experience, you *can* succeed in writing, producing and selling your book—and you *can* make a profit, too. But this is only if you offer quality and make sensible choices at every step. This is where *10 Steps to Publish and Succeed* can help you.

What this book will tell you

10 Steps to Publish and Succeed is divided into three sections:

- Part One is about perfecting your book: publishing essentials, editing, interior book design, cover design, proofreading and graphics (illustrations and photos).
- Part Two is about production: preparing your book for print, fulfilling orders, distribution, e-book creation, marketing and promotion.
- Part Three presents information about the author and her work with writers and publishers.

Each chapter has multiple subheads that tell you the topic of discussion at a glance. This organization enables you either to read about the publishing industry from start to finish or to quickly find the specific information you need.

Every aspect of writing and publishing is creative. It is a learning experience that can teach you about yourself and give you a tremendous sense of satisfaction. Writing unleashes much of what you already know—but it also has so much more to give, both to the reader and the writer.

Dig and develop your talent. You will reach your goal! You will get your book written—and published!

Part I
Perfect Your Content

People who *see* your book should say,
"Yes! I want to read this!"

1

Publishing Basics

First Things First

I F YOU ARE AN INDEPENDENT PUBLISHER, FOLLOWING the guidelines below is essential. This short introductory chapter will help you start on the right foot to succeed in your publishing goals.

Your publisher name

Choose a publisher name that you will be able to use not only with your current book, but also with any others you write in years to come. Your book title should reflect the content of your book (see page 41 about choosing a book title), but the publisher name should allow you to publish any genre. Registering the name with your state or province is a simple and inexpensive process, and in many places, everything can be done online.

ISBN

Obtain your own ISBN for any book you publish independently. ISBN stands for International Standard Book Number. This number is unique for every published book, regardless of the language in which it is written or the country in which it is produced. You will need one for a softcover book, another for a hardcover and another for an e-book edition of the same title. If you make major changes and release a new version of the book, give it a new ISBN. Each new title needs its own unique numbers.

The numbers in an ISBN indicate the country of publication, the publisher and the edition of every title. It is important that you get your own ISBNs with your own unique publisher number. Don't use an ISBN provided by an acquaintance or company that provides one for free or for purchase, because the number will indicate that that person or entity is the publisher. Using a number from someplace else compromises your autonomy as a publisher, even though you bear the costs of publishing.

- American publishers should contact Bowker, the authorized US supplier of ISBNs. To start, it is best to buy a book of 10, available at isbn.org. There is a fee for ISBNs in the US.
- Canadian publishers should write to the ISBN Agency, which is a division of Library and Archives Canada, or visit collectionscanada.gc.ca. Specify the number of ISBNs you need. ISBNs in Canada and most other countries are free.
- Publishers in each country should contact the appropriate national department or authority.

Register for ISBNs using your **publisher name**. If you do not have a business name, it is best to create one first, as changing the registered name later might be complicated.

The ISBN is printed on the copyright page. It also goes in the bar code on the back cover of printed books. Your book designer will be able to provide an accurate bar code. Check with him or her before you purchase a bar code elsewhere.

Some of my clients have asked about the **ASIN**. This is an Amazon number which is provided automatically when you make your book available for purchase there, just as any seller might give an inventory number to a product.

Don't be fooled!

The phrase "self-publishing company" is a misnomer. Either you can publish independently—a term I prefer to "self-publish"—or you may be published by someone else, such as a traditional publisher. If you get an ISBN from a **vanity publisher** (also sometimes referred to as a self-publishing company), the number will indicate it to be the publisher of your book, which can have negative consequences when the time comes for marketing and promotion.

I strongly advise first-time publishers not to engage the services of a vanity press. Depending on which package you sign a contract for, you are assigned service providers for editing and layout whose experience and reputation you don't know. Often you are not permitted to communicate directly with them, but rather, must discuss every issue with an intermediary sales representative. There can be errors and misunderstandings, and you will not be able to figure out whether the problem lies with the sales representative, the person doing your work or the company as a whole. Several people have come to me for help, frustrated and on the verge of giving up their publishing dreams because of the time and money they had wasted trying to make a failing "self-publishing package" work.

If, on the other hand, you choose all your own service providers, such as an editor, book designer and e-book formatter, you will be able to communicate directly with them, and each will have a professional interest in the success of your book that will benefit you both. Whether you hire professionals, engage a vanity press or buy a "self-publishing package," you will be bearing the costs of independent publishing. But your product stands to be better and your journey more enjoyable if you hire people you want to work with who have the skills you need to produce your book in the best possible way.

Setting the date

This books outlines the steps you need to take to produce your book in the best possible way. A word of caution: don't create tight deadlines for yourself. Plan a little more time than you think will be required to edit, design, proofread and print your book.

In any project, factoring in too much time is rarely a problem, but not having enough time frequently is. Eventualities and interruptions can occur. Set dates for post-production events that you are sure you will be able to meet. Your book will be all the more successful for it.

2

Editing

An Investment that Pays Back Abundantly

Y OUR BOOK IS WRITTEN. CONGRATULATIONS! YOU HAVE completed your research, tied all the loose ends and reached the first milestone on your publishing journey.

What next?

First, make a copy of your manuscript. Keep the original for future reference. As you edit, you might delete passages that you will want to retrieve later. Keeping the original copy ensures that you don't lose any material.

Then start from the beginning. Edit. Revise. Polish. When you reread your manuscript, some passages, sentences or phrases will strike you as repetitive, wordy or unclear. You will find underdeveloped ideas that need more detail in order for the reader to grasp your point or apply your technique (in nonfiction); or to imagine a setting or character vividly (in fiction). Correct any errors of grammar and punctuation.

Reread your manuscript several times and ruthlessly make changes to perfect your writing.

Why hire an editor?

Professional editing is an investment that will pay off in many ways. First, you will have a sense of pride in your published book, and you will never feel embarrassed or apologetic towards customers, colleagues, friends and relations when they get their copies.

Not having your book edited professionally can cost you in the long run. If your book is not edited professionally, you could lose good reviews or sales from those who take writing seriously. Bookstores will reject your book on the grounds that it doesn't meet their standards. You may lose opportunities to collaborate with other writers to sell your books. You might write something you didn't mean and see it quoted. The reader might have difficulty understanding what you have written and stop reading your book. You will not get the word-of-mouth recommendations that you might otherwise get.

After all the time and effort you put into writing your book, make sure the production doesn't suffer because you skipped the editing.

Professional editors are familiar with universally recognized stylebooks. For American style, these include *The Chicago Manual of Style, The Associated Press Stylebook and Briefing on Media Law* (commonly referred to as the *AP Stylebook*), and specialized style manuals for research papers, medical books, legal books and technical books. For British style, the most commonly used style manuals are *New Hart's Rules: The Handbook of Style for Writers and Editors* and the *Oxford Style Manual.* There are many other important reference books for editors, including dictionaries and books dedicated to English grammar and usage.

Whether you submit your manuscript to a traditional publishing house or self-publish, you want it to be the best it can be. Traditional publishers used to engage in-house editors to work with writers they decided to publish. Today, if they think a book needs to be edited, they tell the writer to hire a competent editor and then resubmit. Acquisitions editors are swamped with submissions, and it typically takes them from four to eight months to make a decision. A rejection or request for a rewrite is lost time for the author, so it is best to have your manuscript edited before you submit. On the other hand, if you are publishing independently, you cannot afford to have mistakes or omissions that brand your book amateurish after publication. Your writing must not have grammatical errors, logistical flaws, incorrect usage, poor style or embarrassing blunders or gaffes. Even typos are criticized in book reviews if they distract the reader.

To avoid such pitfalls, it is essential to have your manuscript edited by a skilled editor. Every writer needs an editor—even a great writer! As an author, you will want to engage a professional whose eye is trained to find any major and minor writing errors and weaknesses. He or she will correct them or, in some cases, flag them so you can revise your work. You want to publish the very best book possible to make a good impression on your audience and establish a solid foundation for your writing career.

If you find a good editor, don't let oversensitivity work against you. Remember that your editor wants you to succeed. He has a professional investment in your work and knows that your success enhances his own.

I am fortunate to have had wonderful, talented clients. Many of them want not only to have their work polished, but also to learn and improve their writing skills. Having their book edited becomes an educational experience for them, and they can apply what they learn in subsequent work. One client said, "… [Jill's] editing services have proven invaluable, not just for the specific books she worked on, but also because of how much I learned…. The education I have gained has made me a better writer going forward."[4]

An experienced editor is not married to a single writing style, genre or target age group. He or she might edit fiction, educational nonfiction, memoirs, history, spiritual books and self-help manuals. Some editors can even help improve poetry. If you have written a medical, legal, technical or scientific text, you will have to engage an editor who is familiar with the technical terms of that field. If you find an editor who looks promising, but you are unsure about whether he or she is familiar with the genre of your book, just ask.

What an editor does with your manuscript

The editor makes changes based on his experience and language skills—not just the rules of grammar and punctuation. He always keeps in mind the target audience, the author's intention and the author's voice.

There are three levels of editing. An editor will review your manuscript and recommend the depth of editing he thinks it needs. Then you and your editor should decide on the scope of the project together. Once you agree to the terms of the project, the editor will complete the work and send you an edited Word document that has "track changes" turned on so you can alternate between the original view, the marked-up view and the final view. He may also send you a clean copy with all changes accepted, which will be easy to read.

Three levels of editing

The editor makes changes based on his experience and language skills— not just the rules of grammar and punctuation. He always keeps in mind the target audience, the author's intention and the author's voice.

- **Developmental editing**, also called **content editing**, improves the structure of your manuscript. The editor may rewrite passages and move paragraphs. In nonfiction, the edit covers logic, content development and the progression of the work as a whole, from the introduction to the main body and the summary. In fiction, it analyzes the plot, character development, logic, storyline and conflict; the beginning, middle and resolution; and the balance of narrative, dialogue and action. The editor queries the author and advises him to rewrite sections wherever necessary.
- **Substantive editing**, or **line editing**, refines the language and checks the syntax (sentence structure) of your work. It eliminates wordiness; checks the use of metaphor and simile; and works with the passive and active modes. Sentences and paragraphs may be revised, rewritten or combined, though large organizational changes are more often part of a developmental edit. A substantive editor turns a writer with a good idea into a good writer or professional author.
- **Standard editing**, also known as **copyediting**, corrects errors of grammar, punctuation and spelling.

In a published book, the author is responsible for the accuracy of his work. If your book needs **fact-checking**, discuss this with your editor from the start. The edit of a manuscript with numerous references, names, dates and places should include fact-checking.

How to find a good editor

Ask the following questions to ensure that the editor you pick is competent and suitable for your project:

- Has he or she worked on books written in the genre of your manuscript?
- Do past clients praise and recommend his work?
- Will he provide a short sample edit if you request one? (Two pages should be sufficient.)
- Once the edit is complete, will the editor discuss the changes and suggestions he has made if you have questions about them?
- Is the editor's communication with you clear from the start?
- Do you feel comfortable with the editor based on your correspondence or conversations?

To find out more about a particular editor, do an Internet search using his or her name. Read his website, as well as other sites that provide information about him. Have clients or other publishing industry professionals endorsed his work? Can you find an interview of the editor on a website or podcast? Check his profile and recommendations on LinkedIn (linkedin.com) or other professional networks.

How long is a sample edit?

According to publishing industry standards, one page has 250 words. This word-count eliminates discrepancies caused by variations in page size, margin size, font and font size, line spacing and so on. A sample edit of 500 words should be sufficient for you to determine whether the editor can improve your book. The passage should be from the middle of your manuscript, because that section often reveals more about the writing than the beginning or end. A sample edit will not only give you a good sense of the editor's capabilities, but it will also give the editor a good sense of what your book needs.

How many times will the editor read my manuscript?

Usually, an edit includes two "passes." The editor will read and edit the manuscript once, making changes as needed. Then he will read from the beginning again, checking the changes he has made and fine-tuning. Verify this with your editor at the start. It's important for the editor to complete one pass to get the full picture of your book. Then, when he goes through the manuscript a second time, he can ensure that the beginning, middle and end have no inconsistencies of style, no untied threads and no gaps or omissions.

When you review the editor's suggestions and changes, you might be inspired to write new passages or to add or delete text. If your revision is extensive, your manuscript will likely benefit from a second edit. Sometimes, especially after a heavy first edit, a light follow-up edit is worthwhile. If your book doesn't need a complete second edit but you do add passages, it's best to arrange with your editor to read those new passages to be sure that they are consistent with the rest of the book and that you have not introduced new errors inadvertently.

Editing children's books

Children's fiction and nonfiction may be for readers ranging from very young children to young adults. Each age group has its own set of parameters.

In addition to checking the grammar, punctuation, and sentence structure, your editor should be aware of age-appropriate vocabulary and the recommended sentence, paragraph and chapter length. Even the recommended total word count of a manuscript depends on the target age group. Certain topics or subplots are appropriate for young adults but not for middle grade readers. Editing rhymes requires special skills to ensure that the meter, rhyme and stress are correct.

Your editor will make changes as needed for the target age group of your book.

Rates and terms

There are two ways that editors bill for their work: by the project or by the hour. Some editors are willing to work with either arrangement. Others prefer one system over the other.

The advantage of hourly rates is that you will know at the end exactly how many hours were needed for your project. The disadvantage is that you won't know in advance what the bill will be.

The advantage of a project rate is that the amount and terms are set in advance, and whether the work takes a little longer or a little less time than expected, the price will not change. There are no surprises with a project rate.

In my experience, most publishers and authors prefer a project rate established at the start for long manuscripts. An hourly rate can work well for short passages or articles. Some high-end corporate clients use an hourly rate for all projects.

The terms of the agreement with your editor include various elements, for example:

- how payments are made, such as by check, credit card, PayPal or wire transfer
- what percentage is paid in advance and whether there are installments (usually for a project that is expected to take many months)
- the estimated time frame for completion of the work
- the number of copies of the printed book to be sent to the editor

Clearly establishing the rates and terms at the start is essential to ensure that author and editor both know what work is expected. Some agreements are made with a formal signed contract. Others simply use email agreements. Either way, the terms should be clear, complete and in writing.

Preparing your manuscript for an editor

When you decide to send your manuscript for editing, prepare a clean Word document that has the title and word count on the first page, along with your name, address, phone number and email address. Use a standard font, such as Times New Roman, 12 point, and make the type black. The page setup should have one-inch margins on all four sides. Indent the paragraphs. Use 1.5 or double spacing. If your manuscript has subheads, make sure they stand out by putting them in bold or bold italics or by making them two points larger than the running text.

Final words

Your editor will be part of your team, and you will both want your book to succeed. Having a clear understanding of what work the editor will do and on what terms will benefit your book, you and your editor.

3

Proofreading

Catch the Typos before They Catch You

PROOFREADING IS ESSENTIAL AFTER EDITING. IT SHOULD be done before you send the manuscript to a book designer if you are publishing independently, or before you submit it to an acquisitions editor at a traditional publishing house. If you do not have the time or ability to proofread, hire a professional. Your editor may be able to proofread for you or to refer someone.

A proofreader reads the manuscript carefully line by line, looking out for omissions, typos, errors, formatting inconsistencies and any writing issue he or she feels needs to be addressed. You will save time and money and spare yourself from frustration and disappointment later by perfecting your text at this stage.

Proofreading is a task you may be able to do on your own. Read your book aloud to make sure you don't miss a word. You must be able to spot small errors and inconsistencies. Compile any questions that arise during the proofreading process and check them with your editor.

Avoid cutting corners on the fine points. You won't want to be disappointed with your book because of small errors that you glossed over during production. You will want to revel in the sense of pride and fulfillment.

The difference between editing and proofreading

Sometimes the words "proofreading" and "editing" are used synonymously, so it's best to check your definitions with the person you hire. Like an editor, a proofreader will send you a detailed written description of what his or her work will cover. Always make sure that you understand the job description and ask any questions that arise.

Proofreading must be repeated when the typesetting and cover are done. Read Chapter 7 to learn about proofreading a finished book interior and cover.

4

Interior Design and Typesetting

For Your Readers' Ease and Pleasure

A GOOD INTERIOR BOOK DESIGN WILL BE balanced, harmonious and visually appealing. It will reflect the content and make it a pleasure to read.

Your book designer can help you throughout your book production. He understands how to take your text and images from their original, raw state to design, typesetting and print. He makes your book a cohesive whole that is both attractive and technically sound. Your book designer is also your go-to person if your printer, distributor or sales strategist has specific needs for your book.

The interior book designer considers your book's audience, subject matter, ambience, word count and budget. The professional designer is the packager who not only makes your book a pleasure to read—even admired and emulated by other designers and book publishers—but who can help make your book stand out from the competition in the marketplace.

What are interior book design and typesetting?

An architect designs a house so those who live in it are comfortable. A landscaper plants flowers and builds walkways to make a beautiful garden. An interior decorator creates the ideal atmosphere inside a home. All these professionals have the skills and tools to create the best possible outcome for their clients. In the same way, a book designer enhances your book and pleases your readers by choosing fonts, styles and design elements that result in a top quality publication. He has experience, typographical knowledge and design skills, and he knows how to use page layout and image modification software (such as Adobe InDesign, Photoshop and Illustrator) to optimize his capabilities.

Sometimes an inexperienced writer thinks, "I can make headings in Word, set the margins, run a spell check and send the file to the printer. Presto! My book will be printed and ready for the world." However, using your word-processing software's default fonts and centering your headings in bold type will not make your book look professional. Programs such as Microsoft Word (which is excellent for writing and editing) or Open Office Writer do not offer the layout tools and design options that dedicated book publishing and image modification software provide. It takes time to learn these programs and use them skillfully. A book interior should be *designed*.

Interior book design is the art of laying out a manuscript. It is a skill that evolves through experience and by staying up to date with the trends and technologies used for design and printing. At a glance, booksellers, distributors, publishers, librarians, printers and readers can see the difference between an amateur and a professional book design. A small publisher with a substandard product can suffer negative reviews, minimal sales and considerable embarrassment. Fixing the problem can be expensive and stressful.

Why is interior design vital for your book?

People read for entertainment, to learn something or to improve their lives. When a new title catches a shopper's eye in a bookstore, he picks up the book for a closer look. In a matter of seconds, he decides whether to look further it or put it back, sometimes without reading a word! In fact, studies have shown that the magic number is six seconds to make a favorable impression.

If your title appeals to people, they will flip through the pages or click on the search-inside feature of an online bookseller. If the words look crowded and congested, if the lines have rivers of space between them, if the margins are too tight or the text is not justified, you will lose some otherwise interested readers. No one wants to struggle to read a book because the type is too small or too dense or the spacing is poor. Everyone has enough stress already. Reading should be a pleasurable experience.

Some aspects of good typesetting may not even be noticed—which is exactly how it should be. A skilled typesetter makes your content look seamless on every page.

Book design and the reader

Who is your target audience? Knowing who the majority of your readers will be is important for a book designer. Self-help books, novels, travel guides, screenplays, picture books, how-to books and cookbooks all require different considerations and planning. Whatever the genre, the layout should harmonize with it.

A guide for car mechanics should not look like a book on how to plan your wedding. A computer manual should have a simple, clean layout, while the mood of a devotional or spiritual book is enhanced by an ornate design with a script font. A self-help book with multiple subheads, callouts and graphics needs a well-spaced, well-defined design, perhaps with complementary serif and sans serif fonts. The design of a book on Renaissance art must enhance the pictures, while a cookbook needs a layout that makes it easy for the home chef to follow the recipes while cooking.

Seniors tend to need reading glasses; if seniors are your target audience, the typography should ensure that your book is legible for them. An adult novel or self-help book will have a smaller font than a children's book.

For children's books, knowing the appropriate font options for different age groups is paramount. Sometimes quirky, poor quality fonts can be mistaken for cute kids' fonts. Picture books, easy readers, middle grade books and young adult fiction and nonfiction call for different design choices. For a ten-year-old to read a novel without difficulty, the font, font size, line spacing and margins need to be decided carefully. A large-format children's picture book has other requirements.

Does your book target a professional niche or people with a hobby? Does it target a particular age group or gender? Or is it designed to

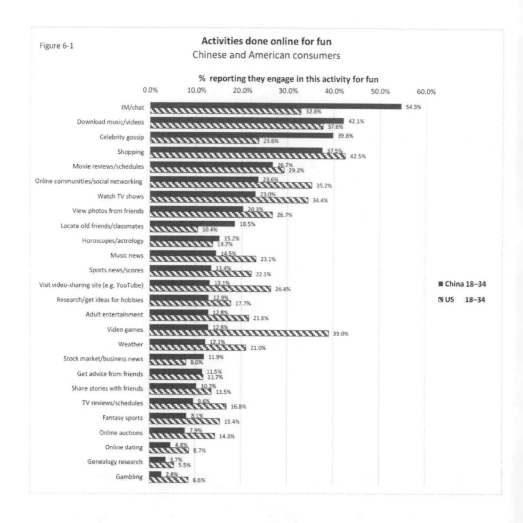

Figure 6-1

Activities done online for fun
Chinese and American consumers

% reporting they engage in this activity for fun

Page 28 shows an original Excel chart provided by my client. Page 29 shows the same chart, designed and formatted to present the data in a clear, attractive way that fits on a book page with a trim of 6 x 9 inches. The comparison illustrates how charts can be designed to make the content easy to read, attractive and consistent with the design of the book in which they appear. Note the larger type, better spacing and clearer contrast of black, gray and white. (This chart was published in Understanding China's Digital Generation *by Heidi Schultz, Martin P. Block and Don E. Schultz and is reprinted here with the permission of Prosper Publishing.)*

FIGURE 6-1: ACTIVITIES DONE ONLINE FOR FUN
◆ CHINESE AND AMERICAN CONSUMERS

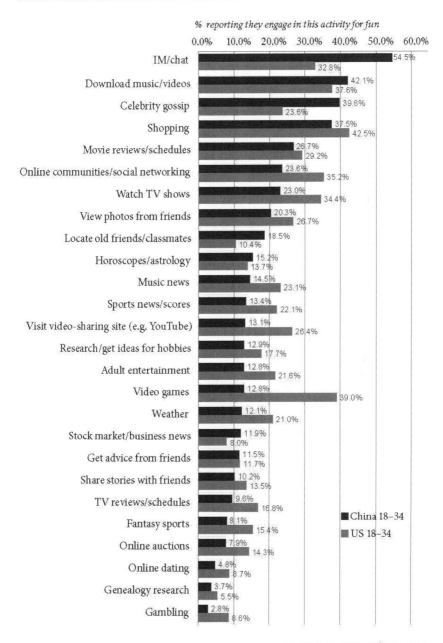

% reporting they engage in this activity for fun

Activity	China 18–34	US 18–34
IM/chat	54.5%	32.8%
Download music/videos	42.1%	37.6%
Celebrity gossip	39.8%	23.6%
Shopping	37.5%	42.5%
Movie reviews/schedules	26.7%	29.2%
Online communities/social networking	23.6%	35.2%
Watch TV shows	23.0%	34.4%
View photos from friends	20.3%	26.7%
Locate old friends/classmates	18.5%	10.4%
Horoscopes/astrology	15.2%	13.7%
Music news	14.5%	23.1%
Sports news/scores	13.4%	22.1%
Visit video-sharing site (e.g. YouTube)	13.1%	26.4%
Research/get ideas for hobbies	12.9%	17.7%
Adult entertainment	12.8%	21.6%
Video games	12.8%	39.0%
Weather	12.1%	21.0%
Stock market/business news	11.9%	8.0%
Get advice from friends	11.5%	11.7%
Share stories with friends	10.2%	13.5%
TV reviews/schedules	9.6%	16.8%
Fantasy sports	8.1%	15.4%
Online auctions	7.9%	14.3%
Online dating	4.8%	8.7%
Genealogy research	3.7%	5.5%
Gambling	2.8%	8.6%

■ China 18–34
■ US 18–34

Source: ProsperChina.com

entertain? Whoever your target audience may be, your book design should resonate with them.

Elements of book design

Book design includes the treatment of text and images. **Typography** is the arrangement and appearance of printed matter on a page. The art and technique of composing type is a critical element of book design and production.

Typography pundit James Felici says, "The rules of typography are centuries old, and although the technologies have changed, the goal has always remained the same: beautiful settings in the service of a pleasant and fruitful reading experience."[5]

Below are some of the main elements of interior book design and typography that a publisher should know, and which a book designer manipulates to make the interior of a book balanced, attractive, legible and harmonious with the subject matter and cover design:

- trim size (page size)
- margin size
- font selection and design for chapter titles and numbers
- font selection, point size and leading for body text
- font selection for section headings and subheads
- drop caps (the large or stylized first letter of the first word in a new chapter)
- front matter: title page, copyright page and table of contents design
- back matter: glossary, appendices, bibliography, index
- running headers and footers
- folio design (page numbers)
- kerning and tracking (letter and line spacing)
- hyphenation control
- orphan and widow control
- graphic elements (photos and illustrations)
- footnotes and end notes
- white space
- use of color or shades of gray
- tables and charts

Most of the terms in the list above are explained on the following pages of this chapter.

Your book may have other design elements, too:

captions	describe or title graphics, charts and tables
callouts	highlight specific points in the text
pull-quotes	repeat key sentences or phrases

These must all be carefully planned, and the book designer can draw from his experience to present you with a variety of options. Borders, tinted backgrounds, shadowing and color are some of the other tools used to create a unique look that harmonizes with your book's subject and target audience.

Typesetting

Your book designer will select a few pages of your manuscript to provide you with two or three designs to choose from. The designs will show different looks for your chapter numbers and titles, body text and running headers. When you have chosen and finalized the design, the typesetting begins.

Typesetting is the consistent application of the design to your book as a whole. It balances the content of every page. It refines the text by using tools and adjustments such as:

tracking	adjusting the spacing of characters on a line or in a paragraph
kerning	adjusting the spacing between two characters
point size	the size of the type chosen for different parts of your book, such as body text, chapter headings and so on
leading	the distance between the bottom of a line and the bottom of the line above it

drop cap	a large first letter of a paragraph, which usually uses the space of two or three lines, and which may be in a distinctive or ornate font
hyphenation control	ensuring prudent use of hyphenation
orphan and widow control	ensuring, for example, that the top of a page does not have the last word of a paragraph
folios	page numbers, which need to be styled and positioned

The book designer considers many other elements of typography that don't need a reference here. Good design and typesetting can make a book beautiful, powerful and appealing. They also help the words flow right into the mind of your reader.

Tables and charts

Tables and charts are modes of presenting data and information so they can be quickly grasped. When well formatted, they are eye-catching and attractive. They are commonly used for material such as glossaries, recipes, price lists, scientific data, statistics, schedules and calendars.

Data for charts and tables is usually saved in Excel, PowerPoint or Word files, which the book designer formats and fits on the pages of a book. He chooses different fonts and type styles to distinguish headers from data. He applies textures, colors or shades of gray to separate rows and columns. An assortment of solid, dotted or dashed lines may be used in graphs.

Typesetting complex charts and tables requires meticulous attention to detail to achieve a uniform look that harmonizes with the book as a whole. Misaligned content or uneven rows look particularly sloppy in print and in e-books. Carefully typeset tables and charts are symmetrical, balanced—even beautiful.

Pages 28–29 show an unformatted chart and the chart as it appeared in my client's book after the design and typesetting were done.

The difference between a graphic artist and a book designer

Graphic artists work with type and images on branding, advertisements, product packaging, brochures, logos, banners and other promotional materials. They predominantly use image-editing software, such as Adobe Photoshop or Illustrator, and the printers they work with specialize in the production of promotional materials.

Book designers use desktop publishing software to format the long text blocks (hundreds of pages) and images that are found in books. They are familiar with the requirements of book printers and binderies.

Different book designers have different levels of experience with graphics, but their primary work is to lay out all the content of a book in a uniformly balanced page design, incorporating book industry standards. Their finished work is a cohesive, technically sound collection of files that adhere to the submission guidelines of book printers.

All the parts of your project come together through your book designer as you traverse the hurdles and revel in the joys of publishing.

Choosing the trim size

At the production stage, the first decision to make—before you begin the interior or cover design—is your book's trim, or page size. Changing the trim after the interior or cover work has begun can be time-consuming and costly.

Choose a standard size. If you start with non-standard measurements, your printer is likely to tell you that their machinery cannot print that size, particularly if you are producing fewer than 500 or 1000 copies through digital printing. If the printer agrees to manufacture a book with a non-standard trim size, the cost will be much higher than usual, because non-standard sizes cause considerable wastage of paper and the presses have to be custom set.

On the following page are some common trim sizes. It is best to check your printer's capabilities before deciding on the trim size of your book.

North America (inches):

Fiction & Nonfiction	Workbooks & Picture Books
5 x 7	7.5 x 9.25
5 x 8	7 x 10
5.25 x 8	8 x 8
5.5 x 8.5	8 x 10
6 x 9	8.25 x 11
	8.5 x 8.5
	8.5 x 11

United Kingdom and Australia (millimeters):

Fiction & Nonfiction	Workbooks & Picture Books
178 x 125	235 x 191
203 x 127	254 x 178
203 x 133	203 x 203
216 x 140	254 x 203
229 x 152	280 x 210
	216 x 216
	280 x 216

Traditional publishers employ book designers. What is the benefit for self-publishers?

Your book will be recognized as a professional product only if all aspects of it—text, graphics, layout, cover and printing—convey superior value to reviewers and readers. An experienced book designer's skills, familiarity with tools of the trade and knowledge of current trends make all the difference.

> ... a well-designed page, like a well-acted performance, looks inevitable, easy. Like anyone could do it—like it's just natural. Until, of course, you try it yourself using Word or some other program with no training or experience. Self-publishers already have to try harder to be seen; if you have

something intelligent to say, good design will make it more accessible, but a cheesy hack job will only help to bury it in the slush pile of obscurity.[6]

—Matt Mayerchak

One of the key criteria of book design is font choice. An self-publisher or new publisher may like a font because he has heard of it. However, fonts have histories, and many have been designed for specific purposes.

Sometimes a client asks me to use Times New Roman for his book because someone recommended it. Times New Roman was named after the British newspaper, the Times of London. In 1929, typographer Stanley Morison was hired to create a new text font, and he supervised Victor Lardent, who drew the letterforms. The font's narrow width allowed more letters, and thus a longer article, to fit in a newspaper column. While Times New Roman is a valuable and reliable workhorse, its closely arranged letters and stylized italic make it less than optimal for books.

Some of my clients have requested that I use Comic Sans for the book cover. Comic Sans is a quality font—so good, in fact, that it has been used prolifically, to the extent that no one with any knowledge of typography will use it anymore, and its use is frowned upon in publishing. Both Times New Roman and Comic Sans are fine for use in your personal projects, but not in books you plan to sell. The point is a professional book designer knows a font's intended use, history, and perception among publishing industry professionals, including publicists and reviewers. He can save you from making embarrassing mistakes that might affect your reputation, book reviews and sales.

Publishers often rely on the book designer to lower production costs by reducing a book's page count without sacrificing quality and ease of reading. On the other hand, sometimes a publisher wants a short book to seem longer, and a skilled book designer can find ways to accomplish this without forfeiting the beauty of the book. The book designer can help the publisher choose the most appropriate paper for the interior and cover, as well as the ideal binding for the genre.

The book designer understands a printer's guidelines and submission requirements and knows what questions to ask if necessary. If a file is not prepared according to the required specifications, what you see on your computer screen or home printout may not be what you get in your book. For every page that must be replaced, printers charge additional fees. The book designer is your best resource to create technically sound printer's files from the start. And if technical issues do arise during production, he will address and fix them.

A printer's **prepress department** puts the designer's files through a set of tests to make sure they have been correctly prepared for printing. If prepress find something wrong, they send a report to the publisher (you—their client) and request corrected files. The publisher usually doesn't understand the report—he just forwards it to the book designer.

📖   TALE:

> Once, prepress at a major printing company contacted my client, complaining about a flaw in the layout of his book. He forwarded the email to me and I checked the files. Immediately, I knew that prepress had made a mistake—the files had indeed been prepared according to the printer's specifications. I telephoned my client's sales representative and asked her to have prepress check again. Within an hour, the sales rep sent me an email saying I was right—a miscalculation had produced a false negative. The files were good, and the book was on its way to press.
>
> On another occasion, a client forwarded a report from prepress that said the resolution of two images in his book was too low. I checked the files and found that the images in question were vector graphics, for which resolution was not relevant. I called and explained the situation to my client's sales representative, who said he would send my message to the prepress department (even though he did not understand my explanation). Prepress understood, and the book kept its place in the production schedule.

One more thing! A professional designer takes pride in his or her work. He never wants someone to pick up a book he worked on, find design flaws and say, "This was done by an amateur." The book designer is your team member, and he wants your book to be the best that it can be.

Better book sales

John Kramer, internationally renowned book marketing expert, says, "... if a book isn't packaged well, it won't sell.... Packaging not only includes the cover, but also the title, the contents, and the interior design."[7]

In a well-designed book, glaring eyesores and design flaws won't jump from the pages and make people think, "I would rather read something else." When people pick up your book, they should say, "Yes! This is a book I want to read!"

The book designer and the back cover

It is common for the interior designer to lay out the text and images on the back cover and spine of a book after the front cover has been completed elsewhere. Once he receives the finished, high-resolution front cover design, he completes the back, spine and flaps (if the cover is a dust jacket) in a harmonious style and color. (See Chapter 5, "Cover Design," for more information about the back cover, spine and flaps.)

Final words

A self-publisher is a publisher. A well-designed book tells readers, reviewers, librarians and booksellers that the publisher values his product. Make sure your book is well-designed and typeset. Access your interior designer's multiple skills and capabilities. This will help your book attain success. You have already put valuable time and energy into writing and editing the manuscript. Produce an excellent book—from text to production. Your book is worth it!

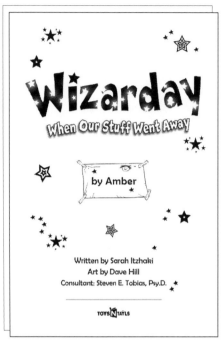

Wizarday: When Our Stuff Went Away

Chapter 6

The Ark

Reilly's parents met him at the airport and he was relieved to see that only Eilam came to welcome him home at the ferry terminal. There was, however, a large banner across Main Street just as he had expected: *Reilly McNamara—2nd Place Winner, National Science Fair*. Below, in smaller lettering: *Congratulations from all of us!* And a reporter from the newspaper called to request an immediate interview. The article was the main feature on the front page later that week. At school the next day Reilly was lauded as somewhat of a celebrity with an assembly in his honor, where he was asked to give full details of the competition. On Friday evening, his parents held an open house at the bakery, where he received tokens of congratulations in the form of

71

Stelladaur: Finding Tir Na Nog

CHAPTER TWO

ORCHANVILLY FIELDS FOREVER

RV and Deluxe approached the edge of a steep cliff that gave them an excellent view of the orchanvilly fields. The scenery below was picturesque: green pastures dotted with flowers, set against a backdrop of white sandy dunes that stretched to the beach. It was a glorious sight indeed! However, RV sensed that Deluxe was nervous. He held her hand as they neared the edge. The sheer height of the cliffs was intimidating and would make almost anyone anxious.

RV was not afraid at all, which was remarkable, considering that he had a wheel beneath him. He was a

17

RV the Racer Aardvark

 CHAPTER 2

Logan Reads the Ten Christmas Rules

"What curse?" I asked suspiciously.

"You know, it's what happens when you publicly say that you don't believe in Santa."

"How do you know?"

"Oh, there's an entire chapter written about it in my dad's old German Christmas book. It's been in my—"

"I know about your book. Logan talks about it whenever I mention anything related to Christmas," I snapped, irritation in my voice.

"Yeah, well the thing's, like, *ancient*."

I shot Tiff a doubtful look.

"Seriously, the book has been in my family for generations," she laughed. "Logan's been begging me since summer to let her read it, but my dad is a little peculiar about letting people see it. You know parents."

11

Catching Santa

Interior pages of children's books. (See page 124.)

Training the Average Person 3

Four-Week Plan

Day	Week 1	Week 2	Week 3	Week 4
Sunday	Family time	Family time	Family time	Family time
Monday	Gym	Gym	Gym	Gym
Tuesday	Spin	Spin	Spin	Spin
Wednesday	Day off	Day off	Day off	Day off
Thursday	Swim	Swim	Swim	Swim
Friday	Date night	Date night	Date night	Date night
Saturday	Mtn Bike Ride	Mtn Bike Ride	Mtn Bike Ride	Mtn Bike Ride

Once you have completed the four-week plan, take a look back and evaluate what you did. Did you complete all the workouts? Did the workouts become easier for you? Did you get stronger and faster? Did you lose weight? Did you do too much, or did you have extra time each day?

*Training the Average Person to Be
an Extraordinary Athlete*

柒

Chapter 7

Digital and Mobile Devices

The marketplace for digital and mobile devices and services in China is a hyper-competitive mix of multinational and domestic brands competing on shifting dynamics of price, distribution, technological innovation and country-of-origin perceptions.

According to the global consultancy R3, two brands that are prominent in the category—Apple and China Mobile—are regarded as the number one and two most engaging brands by Chinese consumers, topping such icons as Nike, Coke and KFC. The R3 study, conducted at the end of the first quarter of 2012, is a proprietary research initiative in which urban consumers are asked to name their favorite brands, recall memorable marketing efforts and identify the values associated with each.

While these two brands are tops for engagement in the minds of Chinese consumers, each faces very different market circumstances in China. On one hand, China Mobile is the government-owned, dominant provider of mobile telecommunications services, with an overwhelming share of the market, as will be discussed later in this

125

Understanding China's Digital Generation

CHAPTER 2

A New Way of Seeing

*In my life I have found that if you expect the best of someone,
they will tend to prove you right.*

—Nelson Mandela

LET'S GO RIGHT TO THE bottom line: *What are your goals as a parent?* Take a moment to think about what you really want.

Ask a group of parents that question, as I often have, and you'll hear phrases like the following:

I want to raise children who are ...
- good human beings
- able to fulfill their highest potential
- responsible
- independent
- successful and happy
- compassionate and kind

I want a family that is caring and supportive.

Most of us share similar goals. How do we reach them? Everything we know about parenting can be boiled down to one fundamental challenge:

21

Bring Out the Best in Your Child and Your Self

Asia 39

**China: North &
Western Asia**

Beijing, Harbin, Kazakhstan, Kyrgyzstan, Mongolia, Tajikistan, Tibet, Turkmenistan, Urumqi, Uzbekistan

Rain & Weather
Rain is heavy in July and August. Northern China has four distinct seasons with winters being cold and dry and summers hot and humid.

Best Time to Visit
China: October (avoid domestic holidays such as Chinese New Year); Tibet, Mongolia: July–August; Northern Kyrgyzstan: June–September; Southern Kyrgyzstan: March–October; Kazakhstan, Turkmenistan, Uzbekistan, Tajikistan: April–June and September–October; Urumqi: May–October

Careful attention to cultural concerns is necessary. Depending on your trip's itinerary, a Multiple Climate pack, page 141, may be necessary.

Weather by Month

MONTH	GENERAL WEATHER CONDITIONS	EXTREME WEATHER WARNINGS
January–March	Cold	WINTER
April	Cool	
May	Warm	
June 1–15	Warm	
June 16–30	Hot, Humid	WET
July	Hot, Humid	
August	Hot, Humid	
September 1–15	Hot, Humid	
September 16–30	Warm	
October	Warm	
November 1–15	Cool	
November 16–30	Cold	WINTER
December	Cold	

Travel-Ready Packing

Interior pages of adult nonfiction books. (See page 124.)

5

Cover Design
Yes, They Do Judge a Book by Its Cover

A S YOU WALK PAST A BOOKSTORE SHOW window, what do you see? When you browse the displays inside, what catches your eye? As you scroll through the pages of a bookseller's website, what do you look at? Book covers! People pull a book off a shelf—or click on a book online—just because they like the cover. As a publisher or author, you want *your* book to be the one they choose.

If the customer likes the front cover, he flips the book over to look at the back. This is prime real estate. Use it to your advantage. Inspiring information and visuals will help your prospective readers take the crucial next steps—buying your book, reading it and then … recommending it to others!

Just choosing an image and plunking the title and author's name on top do not a book cover make! Think of your book cover as a door to a brilliant world. You want your audience to open it and enter to discover what's inside.

Your book title: Capture your audience!

The secret of a successful book title is that it captures people's attention. It may be informative, humorous, poetic or clever, but to work, it should inspire people to want your book. The subtitle is almost as important as the title. It's the author's opportunity to tell the reader more and draw him in. The title and subtitle should work as an effective unit to attract your readership.

The title of a fiction book might be enchanting, sad, scary, serious or intriguing, depending on the genre and target audience. A children's book title might be playful or cute.

Below are some examples of superb book titles. Which of them strike you as informative, humorous, clever or poetic?

Nonfiction:

Presenting 101: For Television, Radio & Events by Rebecca Rifai

The 7 Habits of Highly Effective People: Powerful Lessons in Personal Change by Stephen R. Covey

How To Deliver A TED Talk: Secrets Of The World's Most Inspiring Presentations by Jeremey Donovan

The Changing American Consumer by Marianne Bickle, PhD

Meet Your True Self through Meditation by Swami Shyam

Bring Out the Best in Your Child and Your Self: Creating a Family Based on Mutual Respect by Ilene Val-Essen, PhD

Mind Your Head: An Emotional Intelligence Guide for School Leaders by David Boddy

Men Are from Mars, Women Are from Venus: A Practical Guide for Improving Communication and Getting What You Want in Your Relationships by John Gray

Fiction:

Just One Kiss by Susan Mallery

And the Mountains Echoed by Khaled Hosseini

The Night Is Watching by Heather Graham

The Vampire Hunter's Daughter by Jennifer Malone Wright

The King's Deception by Steve Berry

The Secret Life of Bees by Sue Monk Kidd

Make sure both the title and subtitle achieve their purpose. If they don't, change them. Keep trying different words and phrases until you hit on perfection.

The front cover—the reader's first impression

Once in a while, a new client tells me he has a photo for the cover, so all I have to do is type the title and the author's name, and *voilà!* His cover will be done. I have to inform him that such a cover would only convey that this was an amateur's book that didn't offer much value. Despite the cliché, a book *is* judged by its cover, and book covers are compared to each other.

The front cover starts with an idea. The cover artist may use a photo or illustration as a basis for the design. Colors, shapes, lines, fonts, type sizes and text effects are the tools. Sometimes the image covers the entire cover, and other times the designer places it against a solid color, a texture or another image. Sometimes the title fills the cover if it helps the book more than an image would. If the author is famous, his or her name might be larger than the book title, because that name alone sells books.

The cover design should reflect the content. A children's book cover might have a cartoon—but it won't be political. A book on cooking might have a picture of a kitchen—but not when the sink is filled with dirty dinner dishes.

The fonts chosen for the title and author's name should suit the story or subject of the book. Attraction is the name of the game.

An effective back cover

The back cover should be catchy and serve its main purpose—to maximize your marketing potential. To be effective, it needs a catchy headline, colors that complement the front cover and a layout that draws in and leads the eye.

When preparing the content for your back cover, think of the following elements and discuss them with your designer:

- catchy headline
- concise paragraph or two about the book
- excerpt that informs, excites or intrigues readers
- one or two short endorsements from reviewers or experts on your book's topic
- publisher's name, website address and logo

- BISAC category in the top left corner
- ISBN bar code with a human-readable price at the bottom
- QR code

ISBN bar code, BISAC category and QR Code

These codes and categories serve different purposes.

The ISBN (International Standard Book Number) bar code is required by retail stores because it contains your book's unique identifier and price. It should be on the back cover of a printed book. However, it serves no purpose and therefore should not be on an e-book.

The BISAC (Book Industry Standards and Communications) category at the top left corner of the back cover is used by bookstores to organize stock on their shelves; for example, Nature/Flowers, Self-Help/Motivational or Education/Elementary. A book cover designer can help you choose a category that is suitable for your book. Be sure to use the category name—not the code. The names and codes, which are updated annually at bisg.org, are known as the BISAC Subject Headings and the BISAC Subject Codes.

The QR (Quick Response) code is used to direct traffic to your website or provide the publisher's contact information. See Chapter 10, "Marketing and Promotion," for more information.

☞ TIP:

> You can put a short paragraph about the author on the back cover or the back flap of a dust jacket, with or without a small photo. Alternatively, a section titled "About the Author" can go on an interior page at the start or end of the book. Just make sure it only occurs once. If you include your photo, it should represent you in your best light. It should reflect your brand and the quality should be excellent.

The spine

The title should be as large and clear as possible on the spine, so it jumps out at the viewer from a shelf full of books. Above or below the title, put the author's name and the publisher's logo.

If your book has a hardcover, the spine of the case board (usually navy blue or black cloth) may be embossed with the title, author's name and logo in silver or gold foil.

The width of the spine is calculated when the interior is done. It depends on the number of pages in your book and the type and weight of the paper you choose. This is why the front cover can be designed at the start of production, but the spine and back cover are completed last.

☞ TIP:

>   You may save on costs if you hire your interior designer to lay out the back cover and spine after the front cover and typesetting are done.

E-book covers

Increasingly, publishers release their titles both in print and as e-books. With this in mind, the cover should be designed to display well in print and digitally. This is not difficult to achieve, and your designer or e-book formatter can ensure that your cover is suitable for various devices.

As the digital platform has evolved, e-books have increasingly included not only a front cover, but also a back cover. This gives the e-book a recognizable, attractive ending and it makes the back cover content available to the reader. Read Chapter 9, "E-books and Audio Books," for more information on this subject.

Printing your book cover

The printer's technical specifications for a book cover are precise, and there is no room for error or flexibility. A professional designer knows how to prepare the cover so that there are no problems. If troubleshooting is needed, he or she will be able to address and fix the issues. Cover revisions might be needed if:

- the front cover design is not centered
- the hinge is not taken into account (if the binding has a hinge)
- the spine text is not centered or is too large
- vital elements are cut off in the trim

Choose a designer with wide-ranging experience in the genre of your book. Some cover designers specialize in young adult and fantasy novels. Others work exclusively with non-fiction. Some have a broader range than others. Your designer should be familiar with a variety of printers and should know how to prepare and send files that adhere to their specifications. The beautiful design you see on your computer monitor should translate into a book cover that you are proud of and that your readers enjoy looking at every time they pick up your book.

6

Photographs and Illustrations
Speak to Your Reader Visually

I LLUSTRATIONS AND PHOTOGRAPHS ENRICH THE EXPERIENCE OF the reader. In a memoir or travel book, photos enliven the written words with a face or scene. In children's picture books, illustrations and text play off each other to bring the story alive for young readers. In business books, well-designed charts make complex data attractive and easy to comprehend for the more visual-minded readers.

Several sections in this chapter include simple, useful information, and other sections have technical information that your book designer, photographer or illustrator will be familiar with. Publishers rely on their service providers to ensure that all images meet the required specifications for their projects.

Finding photographs and illustrations

The Internet has a multitude of websites that showcase varieties of graphics, as well as photographer and illustrator portfolios. Some of the well-known sites are Fotolia.com, iStockphoto.com, Sxc.hu, and Gettyimages.com, but there are so many that it is worth your while to explore others, too.

The photography websites have their own search engines. The images have usually been assigned tags or keywords that help you find what you are looking for. Try different search terms to ensure that you get ample relevant results. For example, if you are looking for images of books, search with keywords such as "books," "learning," "study" and "reading."

These websites do not generally display images in the **public domain**. It is best to avoid using images in the public domain for two reasons: there remains the possibility that you will encounter copyright and licensing problems later, which are extremely troublesome and costly if they arise; and Amazon rejects e-books that use images in the public domain.

If you find a photographer or illustrator whose style you like, visit his or her website to find more images that might suit your needs and contact the artist directly to discuss usage rights..

Royalty-free images

When you do your Internet search, key in "royalty-free photos" or "royalty-free images." If an image is not royalty-free, the artist will get royalties on every item you sell that uses that image. This includes books, clothing, posters and other products. Some royalty-free images can be used free of charge, but for most, you pay a one-time fee for the license to use the image in your project. Fees for an image range from one or two dollars to several hundred dollars. To make sure of your rights, read the terms before you download an image and read the section below on "Rights."

Rights

You must have the rights to use any image you include in your book. If you have taken a photo or created an illustration yourself, you own the rights to the image. However, you may need a signed release to use a photo of people in your book, particularly minors.

For royalty-free images that you download from the Internet, rights are granted for **personal use** or **commercial use**. When you make your book available for sale, you must have commercial rights for the images you include.

If you engage an illustrator or photographer, understand and verify all the terms before signing an agreement. Most photographers and illustrators have a standard contract. Clauses can be modified if you mutually agree to a change. Illustrators' agreements frequently include the right to be paid royalties.

Below are basic options in two broad categories:

A.   You own all rights. You may use the image in whatever way you wish—in your book, on your website, in promotional materials (such as bookmarks, business cards, brochures, posters and infographics) and in media productions (television, film, etc.). If you hire an illustrator or photographer and sign a "work-made-for-hire" agreement (also commonly called "work-for-hire"), you will own the rights to the finished artwork. Typically the up-front price for this option is higher than the costs for option B below.

B.   You are granted partial rights by the artist. Understand what you can do with the image(s) and what you cannot do. Websites that offer royalty-free images post the specifics in layman's terms. If your rights are not clearly defined, inquire from the artist or website administrator or try to find another image. For downloadable images on royalty-free websites, the artist grants you specific rights to use his or her work. If you hire a photographer or illustrator, his or her rights must be clearly defined in the agreement you sign. If the work is not described as "work for hire," you are not granted all the rights to the finished work.

Some providers offer images for free that you can use in any way you like—for commercial or personal use; however, most agreements require that you pay a fee for the right to use an image. Sometimes granting of these rights requires specific attribution to the photographer or artist. Abide by all the terms and you won't have any legal troubles later.

Illustrations

Websites with royalty-free images often have an optional radial button or tick box that lets you narrow your search to "photos" or "vector graphics." If you don't specify which you are looking for, you will see both in your search results. Some websites showcase only illustrations and artwork, rather than photos. Illustrations for children's books are done by children's illustrators, and there are websites dedicated to this kind of illustration. (See "Illustrations for Children's Picture Books" below.)

Technically, there are two kinds of illustrations:

- paintings and drawings (pixel-based images)
- digital art (vector art)

Paintings and drawings are usually sketched by the artist and then filled in with color. Often these are done with traditional artist's materials, such as paper, paints, art pens, crayons, and so on; the finished art is scanned and finalized using a drawing or image modification program like Adobe Photoshop or Corel PaintShop Pro. Other times, the artwork is created entirely on a computer with Photoshop or Corel Painter. Either way, the image created is called a **raster graphic**, which means it is made of **pixels** (dots), and the **resolution** (dots per inch) must be correct for print or e-books. (See the section titled "Quality, resolution and size" below.)

Vector art is created in a program like Adobe Illustrator or CorelDRAW. Vector graphics use shapes and colors to create an illustration, rather than painting, drawing or photography and typically have a perfectly smooth edge. Vector graphics can be made as large or small as you like without losing quality.

Quality, resolution and size

If your printer's technical specifications for images are not met, your pictures might look blurry or blotchy in your book. The printer might even reject the images before printing, which could delay your book production. Whether you plan to purchase images online or you have your own pictures, consult with your book designer to make sure the files you want to use will work for your book.

Photos and other color raster images on a book page or cover must be at least 300 **dots per inch (dpi)**. Black line art needs a higher resolution of 600 to 1200 dpi. Images should be crisp and clean—without dust, scratches or other defects. If you cannot clean up your images yourself, ask your photographer, illustrator or book designer to modify them to ensure that they print beautifully.

Always start with an original high-resolution graphic. Sometimes people "cheat" by increasing the dpi of a low-resolution image using image modification software like Adobe Photoshop; this is called **resampling** the image. However, resampling should be avoided in most cases as it might accentuate the defects, rather than hiding them. When you send pictures to your book designer, he or she will be able to ensure that the resolution is correct and tell you if any modification is needed.

The **size** of the original image matters, too. If your book page is 6 x 9 inches and your image is 1 x 2 inches, the picture will be very small on the page. Ask your book designer for help if necessary.

Finding an illustrator

Every illustrator has his or her own artistic style or a portfolio of styles. He may paint with watercolors or acrylic paints; create vector artwork; or draw cartoons or other line art.

For a cover illustration or a single picture inside your book, search websites that showcase illustrator portfolios. Some well-known sites are theispot.com, workbook.com, dripbook.com and freelance.com, but there are many more. Certain websites represent artists from a particular country. When you find an image you like, purchase the license to use it (just as you would purchase the right to use a photo, described above). If an artistic style hits the mark but none of the images you see is quite right, contact the artist and ask if you can commission him or her for your project. Detail your requirements, including how many illustrations you need and what the finished size should be.

If you need multiple illustrations for a story, it is best to have a uniform style throughout that enriches the telling of the tale. For example, many novels have an illustration at the start of every chapter.

📖 TALE:

> Clients frequently ask me to help them find an illustrator. One client wanted pictures scattered throughout her novel, not just at the beginning of each chapter. She searched the Internet and commissioned three illustrators to do a sample line drawing based on a scene in her story. My client and I discussed the attributes of each sample, and she hired the artist that best captured the mood of her book. When the book was published (with almost 30 illustrations), the artist promoted it in bookstores, schools and libraries, furthering her own career while helping the title win several awards.

☛ TIP:

> The layout of your book should be done by a professional book designer, rather than an illustrator or graphic artist. A book designer has experience and the knowledge of page design, typography, software capabilities for book design, best practices for using the software, printer requirements and so on.

Infographics

An infographic is a relatively new kind of illustration that does exactly what the name suggests. It is a bright collage of text (information) and images (graphics) that represents a company or program.

One of my business book publishing clients searched the Internet for just the right cover photograph for a new book, but none of the images she found fulfilled her company's criteria. Finally, she sent me the company infographic. A beautiful full-color vector graphic that gave the viewer a great deal of information at a glance, it was the ideal front cover image for the *The Changing American Consumer*.[8] (See the image on page 53.)

The image used on this book cover is a vector infographic.
(This book cover is in full color.)

Illustrations for Children's Picture Books

Children's picture books require special considerations. Look for an artist or an artistic style in the same way that you would search for photos for your book cover. (See page 47, "Finding photographs and illustrations," and page 51, "Finding an illustrator.") Popular websites that showcase the portfolios of children's book illustrators are scbwi.org/Illustrators-Gallery.aspx, picture-book.com, childrensillustrators.com and picturebookartists.org.

If you are publishing your first children's picture book independently, the steps are similar to the steps for any other book, except that you need illustrations in addition to text. Make sure your story is edited before the illustrator starts, because sometimes an editor will surprise you with a text revision that can change the details of an illustration. Illustrations can be arranged on a page in several ways.

- **Full bleed** pictures cover a whole page or **spread** (the left and right pages that are visible together when you open a book).
- Square or rectangular illustrations may have a margin on each side.
- **Spot illustrations** can be any shape or size on the page.

Discuss your plans with your book designer and your illustrator. The artist will need to know the page specifications before he or she starts to work. Having a harmonious team from the start will help prevent undesirable surprises that either require the illustrator to revise his images or force you to modify your own plans. When technical specifications are not considered from the start, the adjustments can be time-consuming, costly and frustrating for the small publisher.

Traditional publishers have an **art director** who checks the plans and details of the illustrations. Most self-publishers act as art director or ask their book designer to take on this role.

☞ TIP:
> Ask your illustrator for ideas. If he is experienced, he will be able to suggest page breaks in the text that will facilitate the best possible illustrations for your book; this process is called **storyboarding**. Think of him or her as a partner

and resource who wants to create the best possible visual representation of your story. Part of the fun in producing children's picture books is seeing the creativity that the illustrator adds. He might hide gems or cupcakes for children to find in an illustration, or even create a visual story that complements your written story.

📖   TALE:

In one of the picture books I designed for a traditional publisher, the art director asked the artist to hide a different insect on every full-bleed illustration in the book.[9]

The illustrator of another book put a small teddy bear in every picture, even though it wasn't part of the story.

Illustrator's Agreement

Read a few contracts so you are familiar with common terms of an illustrator's agreement. You can find sample contracts online. Attorney Ivan Hoffman has written and posted an article that explains a publisher's agreement with an illustrator. It is worth reading if you have not worked with an illustrator before. (See "The Cover Artist/Illustrator Agreement" at ivanhoffman.com/artist.html).

When your illustrator sends you his contract, read it carefully to ensure that it serves your needs. Most illustrators have a standard royalties percentage in their agreements, usually five percent, and the illustrator retains the copyright of his or her work. If, however, the agreement is work-for-hire, you will own the rights to the finished work; even then, the illustrator should retain the right to use the images for promotional purposes.

The agreement should specify the timeline for completion of the project, the number of illustrations to be completed, the payment schedule, who retains rights to the artwork and how it may be used, and who owns the copyright. The contract should specify which party can use the artwork for other ventures, such as television or movie production. It is imperative that you understand and agree to all the terms of any agreement you sign. To be sure your interests are protected, you may wish to hire an attorney to review the wording before you sign.

☞ TIP:

> An illustrator who retains the copyright on the illustra-
> tions and earns royalties on sales is likely to be excited
> about promoting the book. In effect, he will work on your
> behalf. Someone contracted on a work-made-for-hire ba-
> sis has nothing to do with the book once his or her part
> is done and may be less likely to help with publicity and
> promotion.

Scanning the finished artwork

Full-color illustrations should be scanned as 300 dot-per-inch TIFF
files. Line drawings should be 600 to 1200 dpi without resampling. Since
these files will be too large to transfer by email, the artist can either burn
them to DVDs and send the discs to you and your book designer or,
preferably, upload them to an FTP site from where you can download
them to your computer. There are service providers that transfer large
files for you, most of which are free and some of which charge a fee:
wetransfer.com, hightail.com and transferbigfiles.com are three of the
many websites that provide this service.

☞ TIP:

> Provide your illustrator with specifications provided by
> your designer before he scans the files to ensure that they
> are done correctly from the start. Rescanning all the im-
> ages tends to be time-consuming and frustrating for both
> the illustrator and the publisher. Check with your book
> designer if you have any questions.

7

Proofreading–Again!

Be Proud of Your Book

WHEN THE TYPESETTING AND COVER OF YOUR book are done, you have one last chance to proofread before the files go to the printer. You can hire a professional proofreader or do it yourself. This chapter describes what to look out for while proofreading to ensure that your book is perfect.

Proofreading a Word document was done before the typesetting begins. At this stage, your book designer sends you a PDF to proofread.

How to proofread the interior

In addition to proofreading the text, examine the layout of each page in the book. Check the margins, page numbers, chapter titles, subheads, headers, line spacing, orphans and widows. Make sure there are no rivers (large gaps between words on sequential lines) and that words are not squeezed so close together that you can hardly distinguish them. Most paragraphs should have no more than one end-of-line hyphen, although long paragraphs might have two.

A **spread** consists of the two pages that face each other when you open a book. Make sure the headers are parallel to each other and that the book title, author's name and chapter title in the headers are spelled correctly. Then ensure that the last line of the left page is aligned with the last line of the right page. If they are askew, the spread will not look neat and balanced. Note that every page in the book will not have the same number of lines, but each spread should be balanced.

Check the page numbers in the table of contents against the corresponding pages in the book. Proofread the title page, copyright page, dedication, bibliography, footnotes, end notes and index. The photos or illustrations should be properly placed and sized, and the captions should be correct.

How to proofread the cover

Proofread your entire book cover—the front, back, spine and flaps. Check the ISBN bar code and retail price.

How to list corrections clearly for your typesetter

When you proofread your book, open a new Word document and make a list of the changes you require. Ask your typesetter how he or she would like you to itemize them. For example, for each revision, specify the page number; some typesetters want to know the line number. Even if the only change needed on a line is the addition of a comma, provide at least five or six words from the sentence in question along with your revised version.

Try the following format:

Item	Detail	Text
1.	Page 56:	Sara darted into the yard, picked up the hose and sprayed her brother with unreserved delight.
	Should be:	Sara darted into the yard, picked up the hose and sprayed her **older** brother with unreserved delight.
	Insert:	"older"
2.	Page 103:	The flight leaves at 02:30 from Terminal One.
	Should be:	The flight leaves at **12:30** from Terminal One.
	Change:	"02:30" to "12:30

Another method to record your changes is using sticky notes in Acrobat Reader. As your typesetter makes the changes, the text will **reflow**; for example, if you insert the word "older" in the first example above, the words "brother with unreserved delight" and everything that follows will reflow forward. This is particularly noticeable when several words or sentences are modified.

Editorial changes are generally billed by the hour. Therefore, the more clearly you list the revisions needed, the less time it will take for your typesetter to find the spot in question and make the adjustment, and the more economical it will be for you.

Your book designer will send you a new proof to check. When you decide that no further changes are needed, he or she will prepare the final printer's files.

What can go wrong if you don't proofread after typesetting?

Some people devote years to researching their subject and writing their book. They budget for a riveting cover and an appealing, well-designed interior. However, occasionally, first-time publishers have sent me their manuscript without an inkling that proofreading will be necessary when the typesetting is done. They publicize their launch date without leaving any time for proofreading and editorial revisions.

If you don't take the time to complete this step, you—and your customers—might find errors in your published book. Once people have purchased copies, the damage is done. Reviewers deplore books with multiple errors, and you won't be able to change the reviews once they are posted. You will have sold a product that you could have been proud of, had you taken an extra week or two to proofread.

There is some recourse if this happens to you. You can remove the book from circulation, including all online venues, alter the title, change the ISBN, fix the errors and release the new book. However, if you received any good reviews online, they will apply to the old title, not this one.

If you use a print-on-demand printer (see Chapter 9, "E-books and Audio Books"), you will not have the burden of a large stock of books with errors. Print-on-demand allows you to make corrections, upload a new file (usually for a fee) and release the corrected version relatively painlessly. On the other hand, if you have printed hundreds or thousands of copies, your only option will be to sell your books with the mistakes, give them away or discard them.

Why learn the hard way? Complete every step of your book production carefully, including proofreading, and put your best book forward.

The Way to Wealth

or Poor Richard's Maxims Improved

to which is added

The Whistle
A True Story

&

The Advantages of Drunkenness

Benjamin Franklin

❧Juniper Grove❧

Editor's Note

Though written more than 200 years ago, *The Way to Wealth* contains many timeless adages and bits of wisdom that are still incredibly applicable to our lives today. This edition has been compiled and edited from multiple early copies of *The Way to Wealth* and *The Whistle*, as well as the original editions of several of Poor Richard's Almanacks. A few words have been replaced with their more modern counterparts; as an example, the antiquated "bye-paths" was changed to "bypaths." Some of the more archaic or arcane words have been defined in footnotes.

J.L. Pope

ISBN 978-1-60355-100-7

Contents

The Way to Wealth

———

From 1732 to 1758, Benjamin Franklin wrote the highly successful *Poor Richard's Almanack* under the pseudonym "Richard Saunders." In *The Way to Wealth*, Franklin is again writing as Saunders, who stops at an auction and listens to a speech given by a character named Father Abraham. Phrases that originally appeared in *Poor Richard's Almanack* are italicized within the text.

———

Courteous Reader,

I have heard that nothing gives an author so great pleasure as to find his works respectfully quoted by other learned authors. This pleasure I have seldom enjoyed; for though I have been, if I may say it without vanity, an eminent author (of Almanacks) annually, now a full quarter of a century, my brother authors in the same way (for what reason I know not,) have ever been very sparing in their applauses; and no other author has taken the least notice of me; so that, did not my writings produce me some solid pudding[1], the great deficiency of praise would have quite discouraged me.

I concluded at length that the people were the best judges of my merit, for they buy my works; and besides, in my rambles, where I am not personally known, I have frequently heard one or other of my adages repeated with

———

1   provide a means of living; put food on the table

at the end on't. This gave me some satisfaction; as it showed not only that my instructions were regarded, but discovered likewise some respect for my authority; and I own, that, to encourage the practice of remembering and repeating those wise sentences, I have sometimes quoted myself with great gravity.

Judge, then, how much I must have been gratified by an incident I am going to relate to you. I stopped my horse lately where a great number of people were collected at an Auction of Merchant Goods. The hour of sale not being come, they were conversing on the badness of the times, and one of the company called to a plain, clean old man, with white locks. "Pray, Father Abraham, what think you of the times? Won't these heavy taxes quite ruin the country? How shall we be ever able to pay them? What would you advise us to do?"

Father Abraham stood up and replied — "If you'd have my advice, I'll give it to you in short: for *a word to the wise is enough*; and *many words won't fill a bushel*, as Poor Richard says." They joined in desiring him to speak his mind; and gathering round him, he proceeded as follows:

"Friends (says he) and neighbors, the taxes are indeed very heavy; and if those laid on by the government were the only ones we had to pay, we might more easily discharge them; but we have many others and much more grievous to some of us. We are taxed twice as much by our idleness, three times as much by our pride, and four times as much by our folly; and from these taxes the commissioner cannot ease or deliver us by allowing an abatement. However, let us hearken to good advice, and something may be done for us:

God helps them that help themselves,

as Poor Richard says in his Almanack.

It would be thought a hard government that should tax its people one-tenth part of their time, to be employed in its service: but idleness taxes many of us much more, if we reckon all that is spent in absolute sloth, or doing of nothing, with that which is spent in idle employments, or amusements that amount to nothing.

Sloth, by bringing on disease, absolutely shortens life. *Sloth, like rust, consumes faster than labour wears, while the key used is always bright,* as Poor Richard says.

But dost thou love life? then do not squander time, for *that's the stuff life is made of,* as Poor Richard says. How much more than is necessary do we spend in sleep! forgetting that *the sleeping fox catches no poultry,* and that *there will sleeping enough in the grave,* as Poor Richard says. *If time be of all things the most precious, wasting time must be* (as Poor Richard says) *the greatest prodigality*[2]; since, as he elsewhere tells us, *Lost time is never found again*; and *what we call time enough always proves little enough.*

---

2   imprudence; waste

Let us then up and be doing, and doing to the purpose; so by diligence shall we do more with less perplexity. *Sloth makes all things difficult, but industry all easy,* as Poor Richard says; and, *he that riseth late must trot all day, and shall scarce overtake his business at night;* while *laziness travels so slowly that poverty soon overtakes him,* as we read in Poor Richard, who adds, *Drive thy business; let not that drive thee,* and

> *Early to bed, and early to rise,*
> *Makes a man healthy, wealthy, and wise.*

So what signifies wishing and hoping for better times? We make these times better if we bestir ourselves. *Industry needs not wish,* as Poor Richard says; and,

> *He that lives upon hope will die fasting.*

There are no gains without pains; then *help, hands, for I have no lands,* or if I have, they are smartly taxed; and, (as Poor Richard likewise observes,) *He that hath a trade, hath an estate;* and *he that hath a calling, hath an office of profit and honour;* but then the trade must be worked at, and the calling well followed, or neither the estate nor the office will enable us to pay our taxes.

If we are industrious, we shall never starve; for, as Poor Richard says, *At the working man's house hunger looks in, but dares not enter.* Nor will the bailiff or the constable enter; for *Industry pays debts, while despair increaseth them,* says Poor Richard. What though you have found no treasure, nor has any rich relation left you a legacy? *Diligence is the mother of good luck*, as Poor Richard says; and, *God gives all things to industry*;

> *Then plough deep while sluggards sleep,*
> *And you will have corn to sell and to keep.*

says Poor Dick.

Work while it is called today; for you know not how much you may be hindered tomorrow; which makes Poor Richard say, *One today is worth two tomorrows*, and further, *Have you somewhat to do tomorrow, do it today.* If you were a servant, would you not be ashamed that a good master should catch you idle? Are you then your own master? *Be ashamed to catch yourself idle*, as Poor Dick says.

When there is so much to be done for yourself, your family, your country, and your gracious king, be up by peep of day; *Let not the sun look down, and say, Inglorious here he lies!*

Handle your tools without mittens; remember that *the cat in gloves catches no mice*, as Poor Richard says. It is true, there is much to be done, and perhaps you are weak handed; but stick to it steadily, and you will see great effects; for, *constant dropping wears away stones*, and *by diligence and patience the mouse ate into the cable*; and *light strokes fell great oaks*, as Poor Richard says in his Almanack, the year I cannot just now remember.

Methinks I hear some of you say, "Must a man afford himself no leisure?" — I will tell thee, my friend, what Poor Richard says, *Employ thy time well if thou meanest to gain leisure*; and, *since thou art not sure of a minute, throw not away an hour.* Leisure is time for doing something useful; this leisure the diligent man will obtain, but the lazy man never; so that, as Poor Richard says, *A life of leisure and a life of laziness are two things.* Do you imagine that sloth will afford you more comfort than labour? No, for as Poor Richard says, *Trouble springs from Idleness, and grievous toil form endless ease. Many, without labour, would live by their wits only, but they break for want of stock*; whereas industry gives comfort, and plenty, and respect. *Fly³ pleasures, and they will follow you. The diligent spinner has a large shift*; and *now I have a sheep and a cow, everybody bids me good morrow*; all which is well said by Poor Richard.

But with our industry, we must likewise be steady, settled, and careful, and oversee our own affairs with our own eyes, and not trust too much to others; for, as Poor Richard says,

> *I never saw an oft-removed tree,*
> *Nor yet an oft-removed family,*
> *That throve so well as those that settled be.*

And again, *Three removes is as bad as a fire*; and again, *Keep thy shop, and thy shop will keep thee*; and again, *if you would have your business done, go; if not, send.* And again,

---

3   flee from

He that by the plough would thrive,
Himself must either hold or drive.

And again, *the eye of a master will do more work than both his hands*; and again, *Want of care does us more damage than want of knowledge*; and again, *Not to oversee workmen, is to leave them your purse open.*

Trusting too much to others care is the ruin of many; for, *In the affairs of this world, men are saved, not by faith, but by the want of it*; but a man's own care is profitable; for, sayeth Poor Dick, *Learning is to the studious, and riches to the careful, as well as power to the bold, and heaven to the virtuous.* And farther, *If you would have a faithful servant, and one that you like, serve yourself.* And again, he adviseth to circumspection and care, even in the smallest matters, because sometimes a little neglect may breed great mischief. *For want of a nail the shoe was lost; for want of a shoe the horse was lost; and for want of a horse the rider was lost*; being overtaken and slain by the enemy, all for want of care about a horseshoe nail.

So much for industry, my friends, and attention to one's own business; but to these we must add frugality, if we would make our industry more certainly successful.

A man may, if he knows not how to save as he gets, *keep his nose all his life to the grindstone, and die not worth a groat⁴ at last. A fat kitchen makes a lean will,* as Poor Richard says; and,

---

4   a coin of little value; a penny

Many estates are spent in the getting;
Since women for tea forsook spinning and knitting,
And men for punch⁵ forsook hewing and splitting.

If you would be wealthy, (says he, in another Almanack,)
*think of saving, as well as of getting: The Indies have not
made Spain rich, because her outgoes are greater than her
incomes.*

Away, then, with your expensive follies, and you will not
have much cause to complain of hard times, heavy taxes,
and chargeable families; for, as Poor Dick says,

Women and wine, game and deceit,
Make the wealth small, and the wants great.

And further, *What maintains one vice would bring up two
children.* You may think, perhaps, that a little punch,
now and then, diet a little more costly, clothes a little
finer, and a little entertainment now and then, can be
no great matter; but remember what Poor Richard says,
Many a little makes a mickle⁶; and further, *Beware of little
expenses; a small leak will sink a great ship*; and again,
Who dainties love, shall beggars prove; and moreover,

Fools make feasts, and wise men eat them.

Here you are all got together at this sale of fineries and
knickknacks. You call them GOODS; but, if you do not

---

5   alcohol
6   a lot; a large amount

take care, they will prove EVILS to some of you. You expect they will be sold cheap, and perhaps they may, for less than they cost; but, if you have no occasion for them, they must be dear to you. Remember what Poor Richard says, *Buy what thou hast no need of, and ere[7] long thou shalt sell thy necessaries.* And again, *At a great pennyworth, pause a while.* He means, that perhaps the cheapness is apparent only, but not real; or the bargain, by straitening[8] thee in thy business, may do thee more harm than good. For in another place he says,

Many have been ruined by buying good pennyworths.

Again, Poor Richard says, *It is foolish to lay out money in a purchase of repentance*; and yet this folly is practiced every day at auctions, for want of minding the Almanack. *Wise men* (as Poor Dick says) *learn by others harms, fools scarcely by their own.* Many a one, for the sake of finery on the back, have gone with a hungry belly and half-starved their families.

Silk and satins, scarlet and velvets, (as Poor Richard says) *put out the kitchen fire.* These are not the necessaries of life, they can scarcely be called the conveniencies; and yet, only because they look pretty, how many want to have them? The artificial wants of mankind thus become more numerous than the natural: and, as Poor Richard says, *For one poor person there are a hundred indigent.*

By these and other extravagancies, the genteel are

---

7 before
8 bringing restriction, hardship, poverty

reduced to poverty, and forced to borrow of those whom they formerly despised, but who, through industry and frugality, have maintained their standing; in which case it appears plainly, that *a ploughman on his legs is higher than a gentleman on his knees*, as Poor Richard says. Perhaps they have had a small estate left them, which they knew not the getting of; they think *it is day, and will never be night*; that a little to be spent out of so much is not worth minding: *A child and a fool* (as Poor Richard says) *imagine twenty shillings and twenty years can never be spent*; but *always taking out of the meal-tub, and never putting in, soon comes to the bottom*; then, as Poor Dick says, *When the well is dry, they know the worth of water.* But this they might have known before, if they had taken his advice.

If you would know the value of money, *go and try to borrow some*; for *he that goes a borrowing, goes a sorrowing*, as Poor Richard says; and indeed so does he that lends to such people, when he goes to get it in again.

Poor Dick further advises, and says,

> *Fond pride of dress is sure a very curse,*
> *Ere fancy you consult, consult your purse.*

And again, *pride is as loud a beggar as want, and a great deal more saucy*[9]. When you have bought one fine thing, you must buy ten more, that your appearance may be all of a piece; but Poor Dick says, *it is easier to suppress the first desire than to satisfy all that follow it*; and it is as truly

---

9   disrespectful

Part 2

Publishing and Marketing Your Book

People should *open* your book and say,
"Yes! I want to read this!"

8

Printing Books and Fulfilling Orders

Prepare Your Book for Your Customers

D IFFERENT PRINTERS HAVE DIFFERENT CAPABILITIES AND OFFER a variety of options. The printer for your book must be a "book printer."

You will likely find many local printing companies that produce promotional materials, such as business cards, wedding invitations, announcements, flyers and brochures. Some print on mugs, key chains and T-shirts. Book production is a specialized process with unique requirements, including dedicated equipment for printing, binding, trimming and quality control. Your printer should have experience with and the superior materials required for book manufacturing.

Choosing a book printer

There are several other criteria to consider when choosing a printer. One is the quantity of books you plan to produce. Another is quality. Some printers are known for their friendly and helpful staff and for offering personal attention to their customers. Others are more automated, with less room for adjustment. Total production costs will be affected by the paper choice, the complexity of your project and the location of the printer. When pricing your options, include the fees for packing and shipping your order. You will find a significant range of prices for the same project.

Not all printers produce books with the same level of quality. If the glue is inferior, the binding may crack. If the equipment or staff is not up to par, books may be bound with pages in the wrong order. Delays in production due to printing errors can be extensive, frustrating and costly.

Do your research. Some printers provide bound book and paper samples. If possible, get references from other customers or from your book designer.

📖 TALE:

> Once, a client signed an agreement with a printing company despite their reputation for faulty printing and binding. When he received the printed-and-bound proof, the first forty pages were from someone else's book. The second proof had other errors. Sadly, though he had several titles in mind, the frustration and lost time he suffered due to the ineptness of that printer dampened his desire to publish further.
>
> More minor frustrations can be avoided, too. One client had engaged a reputable offset printer for his first book, but he was annoyed by and dissatisfied with the price and quality of the production. Another client's book had been designed by an experienced and talented cover designer, but his printing company said they could not print it. I recommended a different printer to each client, and they were both delighted with the quality of their printed books, the timeliness of production and delivery and the flexible, understanding customer service they received.

Offset and digital printing

Books are printed using two printing systems: offset and digital.

Offset printing technology, which has been in use for more than a century, transfers an image from the project file (your book, for example) to a rubber blanket and rolls it onto a sheet of paper. The term "offset" is used because the ink is not transferred directly to the paper. Offset printing is efficient for newspapers, magazines, textbooks and large book orders. It produces a high-quality print. Its capabilities include a wide range of papers and inks that are usually used in coffee table books, specialty books, magazines and sometimes children's books. Special papers and inks increase the cost of production.

Digital printing technology began with the computer and started to be used commercially at the end of the twentieth century. It has changed the printing world enormously by making print productions accessible very quickly to many people in large or small quantities, and it has evolved rapidly. The digital printing system transfers the project (your book) to a commercial printer, which reads the information contained in the file. Ink or toner are deposited directly onto the paper. A short print run of up to 500 copies (sometimes up to 1000) uses digital technology, as does print on demand (POD).

Three printing options

Certain printing companies only provide offset printing services for long print runs. Others do only digital printing for short runs or POD. Some companies offer two or all three options.

Long print run: If you are planning a long print run for your book— a minimum of 1,000 to 1,500 copies—it will be done on an offset press. Offset printing is the most efficient and cost-effective way to produce books, newspapers and magazines in large quantities.

Short print run: A short print run—from 25 to 500 books—requires a digital printing system. If you know that you will need at least 25 books or if you think a few hundred copies are sufficient, a short digital print run is the most economical choice.

Print on demand (POD): Print on demand uses digital printing technology. It has several advantages, mostly based on the fact that it allows you to produce a small number of copies—even one. Because of this, you don't have to store hundreds or thousands of books. Each order goes straight to the book printer, who prints, binds and ships that order "on demand." Thus, in addition to printing, the POD printer takes care of fulfillment. There are some disadvantages of POD: the printing cost per book is higher than it is in a long or short print run; it offers fewer paper and ink options than offset printing; and in high-end books (coffee table books, for example) a reduction in quality may be detected.

There are many excellent book printers throughout the world, but a few are mentioned here. For offset printing, check Worzalla Publishing (US), Friesens Corporation (Canada and US) and RR Donnelley (US). For print on demand, the most popular are Lightning Source (US, UK, Australia) and CreateSpace (US). Lightning Source is owned by Ingram Content Group, the largest book distributor to bookstores and libraries in the world. The behemoth online retailer, Amazon, owns CreateSpace.

Black, color and special inks

In a book, text is usually black. Sometimes it is a tint of black (grey) for variation in the design. Either way, the ink is black.

For color printing in the interior and on the cover, the most economical and popular mode is **CMYK**, also known as **four-color**. All the colors in this system are a combination of the basic four: cyan (C), magenta (M), yellow (Y) and black (K). Websites, on the other hand, use a combination of three colors from a color-specification system called **RGB**: red (R), green (G) and blue (B). If your photos, illustrations or text have RGB colors, your book designer or illustrator will convert them to CMYK mode before the printer's files are generated.

Offset printers can print other colors using metallic, fluorescent and other inks. These are usually used in advertising and glossy magazines, rather than in books, because they significantly increase printing costs.

Some books have glitter or other materials glued to the pages.

If you are considering using special inks or materials, discuss your ideas with your printer's customer support representative before signing an agreement. Make sure the cost does not exceed your budget and that any special equipment needed is available at the facility.

Bookbinding

Binding refers to any of various methods of securing the printed pages or **signatures** of a book, usually with a soft or hardcover. A standard signature is 16 pages folded together, though eight pages are acceptable and some digital printers make signatures of only four pages.

Bookbinding is done using various methods (described below) and materials, such as wire, glue, thread, staples, plastic or tape. Dedicated machinery is used to automate the binding process so that large or small quantities of books can be bound quickly.

Perfect binding

Most digitally printed softcover books have **perfect binding**. All the pages or signatures are combined, the edges are flattened and a flexible adhesive is used to attach the printed cover to the spine.

Hardcover binding and dust jacket

Hardcover books are bound with a **case board** made of cardboard and covered with cloth, plastic or leather. Offset printers usually offer a range of colors for the covering of the case board, including black, blue, white and red. Digital printers may offer fewer color options.

Hardcover books are marketed in one of two ways:

- with a printed paper dust jacket wrapped around a single-color case board
- with a printed case board and no dust jacket

After the pages are combined in signatures and sewn together, the case board is attached. The title and author's name can be printed and embossed on the spine in gold, silver or colored foil.

Hardcover books can be **smythe sewn**, also known as **section sewn** and **library quality**. These books open flat and are constructed to last through years of library lending and handling by young children. Children's picture books and textbooks are frequently smythe sewn.

A dust jacket serves several purposes. It conveys a sense of quality to the reader. The flaps provide extra real estate for information that the customer can see at a glance, and they serve as handy bookmarks.

Alternatively, a full-color printed cover can be glued over the case board. This kind of binding is usually used for children's picture books, cookbooks and textbooks, as well as for full-color nonfiction, such as art, photography, travel, nature and garden books. Hardcover children's picture books usually have a matching dust jacket and case board.

State-of-the-art book printing facility ...

... for offset and digital printing

Saddle-stitched binding

Short books and some softcover children's picture books have a **saddle-stitched binding**. After the pages are printed and folded, they are secured with two or three staples down the middle of the fold. The spine is too thin to have any text printed on it.

Spiral binding

Spiral binding, also known as **comb binding** or **coil binding**, utilizes wire or plastic coils to bind the pages; the coils become the spine. The main advantage of spiral binding is that the book lies perfectly flat when open. This is useful for practical, step-by-step guides, such as cookbooks and manuals. The disadvantages are that the book may not have a printable spine, so it cannot easily be identified on a bookshelf, and the binding doesn't lie flat in a stack of books. However, these issues can be overcome by enclosing the spiral in a case board, which provides a hard, flat spine.

☞ TIP:

> Whether you choose POD, a short print run or an offset print run, and whether your book has a softcover, a hardcover or a spiral binding, be sure to get a hard copy proof from the printer and check it before you sign off on the project. Issues can arise, and you will want to catch them before your customers do. Flip through the book, checking the following points:
>
> - Are the lines of text at the top of every page straight and parallel to the trim?
> - Is the type clear?
> - Is the color accurate?

☞ TIP:

> You will save yourself time and avoid frustration and extra expense if you discuss your printer's specifications with your book designer. Do this before the cover designer gets too far along in his work, because changing the art later

can be costly and time-consuming. Your cover designer will need precise measurements before he starts. Your interior book designer holds the reins of your project and can bring together the requirements of the printer, the cover and, of course, the pages of your book.

Costs and Fulfillment

Offset printing has setup fees for technical steps that are not required in digital printing, but the production cost per book is lower than it is in digital printing. If you print a large quantity of books, you will have to make arrangements to store them and fulfill orders. Storage requires a dry space where the books will not be damaged over time, and packaging and shipping can be tedious and time-consuming; therefore, fulfillment is often handled by a third-party service provider. If you do a long print run and engage a distribution company, read the terms of the contract carefully. If there is anything you don't understand, discuss it with your sales representative before signing.

If you prefer to store books and fulfill orders at your home or office, you will need sufficient space, supplies and perhaps an assistant. Before you print a large quantity of books, be sure there is a market for them and that you have a good marketing strategy in place.

Digital printing generally has a higher production cost per book, but it does not have the same technical setup fees. (Setup fees may be charged for other reasons.) It is usually more economical for new self-publishers to print digitally unless their target markets and marketing strategies are well established.

Even before you choose a printer, decide how you want to fulfill your orders. If you print using POD, the printer will handle the fulfillment. You can order your own books and have them delivered to your address. If your books are available for sale at online venues such as Amazon, Barnes & Noble, WH Smith and Abe Books, the orders will be processed and fulfilled together.

9

E-books and Audio Books
Extend Your Reach

T O MAXIMIZE SALES OF YOUR BOOK, IT is wise to make it available in several formats. E-book sales have accelerated since the Amazon Kindle made its first appearance in November, 2007, and they soared with the release of the Apple iPad in April, 2010. The brands and models of e-book readers and tablets keep growing as devices are manufactured around the word, and the sales of e-books keep rising.

Audio books have been around for a long time, but now they are benefiting from the age of technology and are becoming more popular.

Publishers have kept up with the digital age by releasing books, magazines and newspapers in electronic formats. Libraries have developed ways to lend e-books. The whole field of publishing and the activities of reading and learning have expanded, fueled by the global advance of technology.

E-book readers

The e-publishing industry is changing constantly as developers create new devices to suit the needs of publishers, writers and customers. The two most common kinds of reading devices are dedicated e-book readers and multipurpose e-book readers.

Dedicated e-book readers

Dedicated e-book readers display electronic books, magazines and newspapers, and most include an Internet browser and email. Some, such as the original Amazon Kindle, Kobo eReader and Sony Reader, have an e-ink screen (which is easy on the eyes), can be read in sunlight and have a long battery life.

Multipurpose e-book readers

Multipurpose e-book readers have more capabilities. Most have LCD color screens with varying resolutions . These devices are made for reading e-books, Internet browsing, email, note taking and task scheduling. They also include recording and listening to music, photo and video capture and display, business enhancements, games and data transfer. The Apple iPad, Amazon Kindle Fire and Google Nexus are among the most popular.

Converting your book into an e-book: EPUB and MOBI files

If your book has been designed for print, start with the Adobe InDesign file or a high-resolution PDF for the conversion into an e-book. Your book designer may be able to prepare your e-book using InDesign or other software. If not, you can hire someone who specializes in e-book conversion and formatting. An edited and proofread Microsoft Word file can also be used.

The two main file formats displayed on e-book readers are EPUB for most devices and MOBI for the Amazon Kindle. These are what you would make available to customers through online booksellers and your website. EPUB and MOBI files provide for the full capabilities of an e-book device: changing the type size, writing notes, bookmarking, highlighting passages, using the valuable search feature (which takes the place of an index), enabling active internal and external links and looking up words in the device's dictionary. Some e-book readers can display PDF files, but PDFs are not proper e-books; they can be frustrating for the person reading them, because most of the capabilities of an e-book reader, listed above, do not function in them.

EPUB and MOBI e-books can be displayed on a computer if you download the free software needed to view them. To read a Kindle e-book, get Kindle for PC or Kindle for Mac, which are available from Amazon. To read an EPUB file, download Adobe Digital Editions from Adobe.com. Other viewers are also available. The best way to proofread an e-book before you release it for sale is by viewing it on a dedicated e-book reader, but if you don't have one, the programs mentioned above will usually work sufficiently. Note, however, that they do not always display e-books with complex layouts as accurately as your customers' e-book readers will do.

☛ TIP:

> Ask your e-book formatter to run your EPUB through the EPUB validation test required by Apple. The Kobo eReader, Sony Reader and Tablet, Google Nexus and other devices will display the same EPUB file.

Fixed layout

For a book with a complex layout or one that is rich with images, the standard EPUB and MOBI formats might not be ideal. For example, if a picture of horses grazing in a green pasture has the words "The most heavenly place on earth!" on top of the grass, "The skies have never been bluer!" on top of the sky, and "Book your trip today!" right above the horses, you might lose this somewhat complex layout in a standard e-book. If your book depends on the precise placement of the text on the picture staying the same, ask your e-book conversion person to make a **fixed layout e-book**. This will ensure that every page in your e-book looks identical to the corresponding page in your printed book.

While fixed layout is good for complex designs, there are several reasons why it is not suitable for e-books that are primarily text:

- The device's search function will not work with fixed layout, so a person will be unable to search for a term and find its location.
- Text highlighting will not work.
- The feature that allows the reader to make text larger and smaller to suit his vision will not work.
- Most devices can't display fixed layout e-books.

Only the Apple iPad and the Amazon Kindle Fire currently display fixed layout e-books. Other devices may follow their lead, particularly as the demand increases.

Sometimes, modifying the print layout is the best solution for e-book conversion. In the example of the horses, if the only text was "Book your trip today!" you could move it to the white space below the picture and create a standard e-book. The viewer would be able see the picture, read the text and retain the full functionality of his device.

Enhanced e-books

If you would like to have sound and video in your e-book, produce an "enhanced e-book." To include audio, make a high-quality recording and send it as an MP3 file to your e-book formatter. Either read your book yourself or hire a voice professional. Mix in some music if you like. In fairness to your buying customers and to get good reviews, make sure the quality of your recording is superior.

Enhanced children's books have "Read-Aloud" and animation. Children can hear the story as they read the words highlighted on the screen; those who are too young to read can simply look at the pictures while they listen. Sometimes there is an option for children (or someone else) to read the e-book aloud and record it.

Enhanced nonfiction e-books have embedded audio and video clips. These do not have to be readings of the book. They can include other material; for instance, in a guidebook about France, there might be a short video clip of the Eiffel Tower; in a book about the temples of India, there might be a recording of sitar music; and in an e-book about clocks, there might be a slide show on time pieces over the centuries or an animation depicting the inner workings of a clock. Producing an enhanced e-book is a large undertaking: you will have to supply the video or audio files in addition to the regular content of your book. If you are thinking of doing this, find a service provider who has the skills required for the project.

Contrary to what some people think, an enhanced e-book is not an app. Apps require more complex programming than enhanced e-books do.

☞ TIP:

> Always be sure you have the right to use any audio or video clip you put in your enhanced e-book, as you would with quoted text or images. Get permissions in writing.

☞ TIP:

> Your book designer may be able to advise you about the different e-book formats so you can pick the one(s) that will work best for your book.

Why it's best to hire a professional

A professional will ensure that the code in your e-book is clean. Your readers won't find a heading with an incorrect font size, an unseemly large, blank space or a subhead that falls too close to the paragraph above it. Photos and illustrations will be centered and sized correctly for e-book readers.

The code in e-books that are created using push-a-button software can be flawed, and therefore, they may be rejected by Amazon, Apple and other vendors. Vendors that start with a Word document and offer low-cost conversion generally have little quality control: the formatting of your e-book is likely to have errors. Such vendors also offer no protection for your e-book, and some create a "PDF e-book" for sale. A PDF is the easiest file format to pirate and pass around, and if you allow a PDF of your book to float on the Internet, it might end up as a free download from any number of dubious websites.

Pricing your e-book

During the first few years of e-books, most were priced at $0.99. This was because book prices had always been based primarily on the per-book cost of production, and initially, people applied the same measures to e-book pricing. Since expenses such as paper, ink, binding materials, machinery, storage, packing and shipping didn't exist for e-books, the cost of producing them was comparatively inexpensive.

Then pricing started to change because perception about the significance of books changed. People started to put a price on the value of the content and the writer of the content—not just the cost of production—whether the book was fiction, which required specific skills for fiction-writing, or nonfiction, which required research and experience as well as writing skills.

The retail prices of e-books fluctuate from week to week, and there are those in the industry who watch them the way some people watch stock prices on Wall Street. However, in general, an e-book is now priced just a few dollars lower than the same book is priced in a softcover. The large traditional publishers that first entered the forum of e-book production and sales were pioneers in setting prices based on the perceived value of the content. Then successful authors who published independently raised the standard for the value of their books.

At the beginning of June, 2013, the most popular price range for best-selling e-books was from $3.00 to $7.99.[10] In mid-June, 2013, the average price of an e-book bestseller was $9.17.[11] Prices and averages fluctuate, but this demonstrates that you don't have to price your e-book at $0.99 for it to do well.

Two other factors that affect pricing are royalties and discounts. Vendor have their own policies and programs which you, the publisher, will have to agree to in order to sell your e-book through their websites. Each gives a fixed percentage of the retail price to the publisher and sets its own (often fluctuating) discounts for the buyers. Whatever these arrangements may be, you are likely to have more sales through large, well-known, widely trusted vendors like Amazon, Barnes & Noble, Abe Books, Waterstone's and WH Smith than you will through your own website, no matter how much promotion you do. So don't fret too much about the terms.

Think about what the content of your e-book is worth, what it cost you to create it, what your competition is charging and what you think your customers are willing to pay. Then price your e-book.

☞ TIP:

> If you have trouble uploading your e-book to an online vendor's website, ask your e-book formatter or interior book designer for help.

☞ TIP:

> Ensure that you set the same price in all your publisher's accounts online. On your own website, avoid selling your books for less, or you may incur the wrath of the giants and lose your book's visibility on their sites.

Audio books

The popularity of audio books is increasing. People can listen to them on their cell phones, e-book readers, MP3 players and laptops while doing other activities, such as exercising, cooking or gardening. With head-phones one can listen to a book in a waiting room, café or park. Some people with limited leisure time are avid audio book fans, whether their interest is self-help, educational or business, fantasy, romance or general fiction—or even poetry.

Audio books can be wonderful for older people, those who are sight-impaired and people with other disabilities. For people of any age, certain health problems can make printed books and even e-books difficult to manipulate and read.

When you make an audio book, quality is critical. The sound must be clean and crisp. The voice must be appropriate to the content and pleasing to the listener, whether you do the reading yourself or hire a voice professional. Use good equipment so the recording doesn't sound tinny. If you do the reading, sit in a room with the door closed, where there will be no sound of the doorbell ringing, the kids playing, the dog barking, leaves rustling outside your window or traffic moving on the street. Otherwise, you might have to redo your work.

You can mix in a short music clip at the beginning or end of the book, but don't overdo it. Remember that the listener brings his or her own sensibilities to the listening experience—just as the reader brings his own emotional response to the reading experience—and if the music isn't done professionally and appropriately, it could adversely affect the listener's reaction. Edit the final cut using audio software to eliminate white noise.

Are e-books and audio books replacing printed books?

While the popularity of e-books and audio books is growing, printed books are still the most favored kind of book. E-books are, however, a hot topic in the publishing world, with promotion fueled by the e-book makers.

In September 2013, Booktradeinfo.com reported a study of travelers' reading preferences conducted by Heathrow Airport. The results came as a surprise to many. They showed that 71% of travelers would rather pack several printed books in their luggage than a lightweight e-book reader. Books were preferred around swimming pools and on beaches, and 67% said they prefer print books in general because they enjoy the feel of a real book in their hands. More than 1 in 10 (12%) want a complete holiday from technology while travelling.

Do you want a printed book? An e-book? An audio book?

People have different preferences at different times in different places.

They like to read printed books. They can hold them in their hands and quietly read in the living room or garden, in a waiting room, on a plane or curled up in bed. They can put their electronics to bed and make reading a completely separate, peaceful activity. They can borrow printed books from a library or pass them on to others, and no extra purchase of an electronic device to enjoy them is required.

People like e-books. They can store hundreds of titles on an e-book reader, along with their music, videos and magazines. E-book readers are convenient.

People like audio books. They can play them on their e-book readers, MP3 players or other electronic devices and listen while doing other activities.

Why not make your book available in all formats so it is accessible to more people? Every format translates into a passive stream of income for the publisher, and it can remain available to customers for years to come.

10

Marketing and Promotion

Communicate!
A Cornucopia of Possibilities

I F YOU WANT YOUR BOOK TO SELL, you have to promote it. Today, even traditionally published authors must do their own book promotion. There are various ways to do this. Some are time-honored activities that involve meeting people in person. A cornucopia of new methods and opportunities has evolved thanks to the Internet. In fact, the Internet has not only dramatically changed and expanded marketing options, but its very existence enables the development of creative new techniques and strategies all the time.

If you keep up with the trends, you will be able to test brand new methods. Schedule and use as many techniques as possible to build your platform and achieve the maximum reach for your book.

Your **platform** as a published author constitutes all the ways you are seen by and communicate your message to your target audience. Your message is that you have published a book that others will benefit from and enjoy. **Visibility** and **communication** are critical. Your platform is formed by several components, such as your

- Internet presence
- published books and articles
- television and radio appearances

- published interviews
- reputation and credentials as an expert in your field
- experience and qualifications as a teacher
- affiliation with a brand or personality that promotes you and your book
- membership in writing and peer groups

Publicity is a matter of understanding and engaging with other people—networking through writing, speaking, getting to know people and letting them get to know you.

In a word: *Communication!*

When should book promotion begin?

Book promotion starts before your book is released, and it continues long afterwards. Start to build an interest in your book six months to a year before the launch. This requires significant planning. For some people, creating a buzz four months in advance is more realistic. If you have not yet launched your publicity campaign and your book is coming out soon, start now.

Publicity does not stop three months or six months after the launch. You have to publicize and promote your book for a long time to keep it visible to new readers and to generate new sales. Robert Kiyosaki, author of *Rich Dad Poor Dad,* says his book has stayed on the New York Times bestseller list for six years because he never stopped promoting and selling it.

Some writers don't enjoy engaging in publicity. Others do. If promotion isn't your cup of tea, hire a publicist to get your book off the ground. While publicists are not the most cost-efficient way to gain publicity, they do take care of some things, such as writing and sending out press releases and facilitating live presentations, radio events and television interviews. Once your publicist has fulfilled the contract, you will have to pick up the torch and keep the flame burning. Try to make marketing fun for yourself, and engage the help of other people as much as possible.

Traditional publishers used to take care of all book marketing and promotion. An author only had to write and perfect his manuscript, and when it was accepted for publication, he could devote himself to writing the next one. Today, agreements between traditional publishers and authors require that the author do a certain amount of book promotion. Before considering acquisition, a publisher will likely ask the author about his promotion strategy. Authors frequently say they are surprised by how little promotion their publisher does and how much they are expected to do themselves.

You can do many things yourself to publicize your book. This chapter describes activities to engage in and methods to apply before and after the launch. Certain things can be done at little or no cost. Others require the help of a professional. Do as much as you can within your budget.

Good luck with your marketing campaign!

What are book marketing, publicity and promotion?

Successful book marketing is not just about selling. It involves engaging with people in different communities who are interested in you and your book and providing them with quality material. Marketing continues to succeed when you build and maintain a lasting relationship with your audience. For this to happen, you must publicize your book, which means you must tell people about it.

Marketing, in the traditional sense, identifies the customer and his or her need or desire. Then it presents him with a product to satisfy that need. With regard to publishing, your book is the product that provides the information or entertainment that your customer, the reader, needs.

Publicity helps fulfill the need or desire by making your book visible to as many customers as possible.

A **marketing plan** looks at the big picture. Traditionally, it includes the product (your book), the price, the availability of the product (online and offline) and the promotion strategy. Product, price, place and promotion are "the 4 P's." However, a new business model can be viewed parallel to the 4 P's, which many think makes more sense in the light of modern technology and today's customer's approach to shopping. This is SAVE: solution, access, value and education, according to an article written by Gregory Ciotti in January 2013.[12]

Below are some questions to help you chalk out a basic marketing plan. Writing down your answers will help you make choices that work for you and your book.

A. **Product/Solution:** First, look at the appropriateness of your product—your book—for its market. Then think of your book as a solution to your customers' need to learn or desire to enjoy.

- Who is your target market?
- Why do they need or want your book?
- Who is your competition?

B. **Place/Access:** Where will your book be sold? What outlets—online and offline—will buyers visit to obtain your book? Have you chosen easy-to-find locations? Is information about your book accessible not only through online and offline stores, but is information about it (particularly for nonfiction) available through social and professional media? Various distribution channels involve different costs and benefits. You might decide to engage a dedicated distributor to stock books and fulfill orders, or you might sidestep that channel by using a print-on-demand company that takes care of fulfillment. This will depend on your budget and the demand for your book.

 Make a list of venues where your book will be available for booksellers, other retailers and individual customers, and write down your reasons for choosing these venues. Then make another list of places where you could be market your book and write down your reasons for deciding not to use them; you will be able to utilize this list later, when your initial plan is in swing.

C. **Price/Value:** Research other books on your subject and check their prices.

- Not only should you ask how the price of your book price compares to others of the same genre, but what value does your book offer to the reader?
- Should you adjust the price? Why or why not?

D. **Promotion/Education:** Think about promoting your book or about educating people through its content. This consists of two phases:

- **Phase 1** involves getting distribution and industry partners and associates interested in your book. In this phase, explore the available distribution channels and contact those that fit your requirements. Send out press releases, set up interviews, meet people at events and get introductions to industry professionals in different niches. When your distribution channels are set up, customers will easily be able to find places to buy your book.
- **Phase 2** involves reaching out to your customers and readers. This includes publicity on the Internet, radio and television; in magazines and newspapers; and through live events.

Book promotion may include **paid advertising** or **free publicity**, or both, but in order for it to succeed, **networking** is indispensable. In some ways, free publicity is more powerful than paid advertising, because it usually involves communicating with other people. For example, you might network with hosts of blog, podcast or radio shows to reach their listeners; with newspaper or magazine columnists to connect with their readers; or with organizers of live presentations or webinars to meet their audiences. Networking means the word about your book reaches people directly.

Above, I have presented a broad outline of the complex field of marketing. Specific activities and methods are in the next section—what you can do to promote your book. Once you know the options, choose those that are right for you. Decide how much you can do yourself and make a schedule you can follow. Then think about how you can engage the help of others. New avenues for promotion open up constantly, particularly through the Internet, so stay informed of the trends to keep your marketing campaign energized.

📖   TALE:

> One of my clients spent several years and a considerable sum of money writing and producing her book. She engaged me for editing, interior design and cover design, and the book earned five-star reviews from award-winning novelists and readers. I thought the book was so good that I suggested special marketing opportunities that would normally require bestseller list rankings over a sustained period. However, she insisted that since the book was exceptional, it would succeed on its merits alone, and she didn't even make an effort to maximize its first-place awards through active promotion. Eight months after the launch, sales remained dismal, and she admitted that just writing and publishing a great book was not enough. She had to start publicizing and promoting to open the doors to success.

Do it yourself or hire an expert?

How are you going to publicize your book? How will you make it stand out from the competition? Thousands of people might enjoy reading your book or find it useful, but if they don't know about it, they certainly won't buy it.

Start planning your marketing strategy before you finish writing. Be prepared to stick with your campaign for a long time and to work on it persistently.

If you decide to hire a publicist, be sure that he or she comes highly recommended and that you have carefully considered how his work will help you. No publicist can guarantee sales, because many factors are involved: demographics, competition, the state of the economy—even the mood of prospective buyers when they climb out of bed in the morning. However, a publicist *can* give your book publicity and visibility.

If you develop your own marketing plan, hiring an assistant to do some of the work for you might be the most economical and profitable option. An Internet-savvy student could be the perfect person for the job. However, don't hire someone who "blasts" your information across the Internet for a few dollars, because it probably won't work and it might negatively affect your book's rankings on Google and other search engines. Worse, if you are poorly represented—or misrepresented—your reputation and book sales may suffer, and this would be difficult to recover from.

Do at least some of your own marketing. People will want to get to know you, the author and publisher, and to find out why you decided to write your book. Do some form of book promotion a few times a week. Make sure your written publicity has no typos or grammatical errors; after all, you are a writer and people expect you to know how to write properly. Apply as many of the ideas presented in this chapter as possible.

Networking: It's all about people!

Meeting people who can help your book succeed is essential, both in person and online. It is *people* who will be interested in your book. People will buy, read, enjoy, learn from and recommend it.

Call on the team who helped you. If you engaged an illustrator, it is in his or her best interest to see your book succeed. Speak to sellers, media people, colleagues, educators, librarians and service providers; members of online forums, groups and blogs who have writing and publishing interests; book clubs, writers' associations and publishers' groups; friends, family and colleagues—network with everyone, online and in person, and tell them about your book. Before you ask for their help, think about how your book's success will help them and script your request.

Book marketing and promotion are the most powerful when done by people, for people.

Advance Reading Copies and Book Reviews

Respected and verifiable reviewers give your title credibility. Positive reviews help stimulate sales. They tell prospective buyers that people like your book and inspire them to purchase a copy for themselves. Readers' reviews on Amazon, Barnes & Noble, other booksellers' websites and book blogs are also valuable. Reviews contribute to your publicity campaign.

Once you have some reviews, use them to your advantage. Put a succinct excerpt from your most impressive review on the back cover of your book. Use a phrase from a different review on the front cover if it doesn't interfere with the design. Put other endorsements on the first page. Use quotations on your website, in your email signature and on other promotional materials. (However, refrain from copying Amazon readers' reviews, as Amazon may consider this to be copyright infringement.)

Good reviews are a valuable publicity tool that you can use repeatedly and creatively in a variety of ways.

Advance reading copies (ARCs)

One way to get reviews is by printing advance reading copies (ARCs) three to four months before your book launch. The front cover should be clearly marked "Advance Reading Copy. Not for sale." Your book designer will put this and other important information on the front cover:

ADVANCE READING COPY—NOT FOR SALE
Title: Your Book Title
Subtitle: Your Book's Subtitle
Author: Your Name
ISBN: xxx-x-xxxxxxx-x-x (softcover)
ISBN: xxx-x-xxxxxxx-y-y (e-book)
Pages: Number of pages including blanks
Release date: Month and Year
Published by: Your Publishing Company name and address
Website: Book or author's website, or both
Kindly email a copy of your review to the publisher at:
you@your-email-address.com

Do your research online and make a list of reviewers. Use a short-run printer or print-on-demand to produce as many copies as you need, and send the ARCs along with a well-written cover letter requesting a review. Send a copy to your production team members to check the final version before it goes to print.

The cover letter should be engaging and to the point, showing professionalism and respect for the reviewer's time. It should reflect your writing style to give a taste of what's to come in the book. The grammar and punctuation should be flawless. You only have one chance to write an appealing cover letter.

📖 TALE:

One of my clients wrote an exceptionally creative book for children with special needs. He hired a skilled illustrator and engaged me to edit and design the book. Then he prepared his targeted list of reviewers and printed the ARCs, but he took one unfortunate shortcut: he did not have his cover letter edited.

Sadly, the letter had grammatical errors and the content was not optimized for the reviewers he wanted to impress. It did not reflect his ability and hard work or the quality of his book. It was too late to edit the letter and say, "I'm sorry I sent you an unfinished letter with my book. Please replace it with my revised one."

Fortunately, the book went on to win acclaim from experts in his field, but he will never know if he lost a few good reviews because of his flawed cover letter. He certainly would have been a happier publisher had he saved himself from the trauma he experienced by not taking the time to write a great cover letter.

When you send an ARC to a reviewer, the book is his or hers to keep. However, despite the phrase "Not for sale" on the cover, you might find it listed with an arbitrary price on eBay or Craig's List. Don't fret. Look at the bright side! If someone is displaying your book online, people will see it and this may lead to real sales. Your book is getting publicity, even if it's through a less than perfect channel.

How to find reviewers

Traditional publishers have deep-rooted relationships with mainstream reviewers like the New York Times, the Los Angeles Times and the Guardian. It is usually difficult for new self-publishers to pique the interest of these newspapers. However, other reviewers, such as Midwest Book Reviews, Book Pleasures and Foreword Book Reviews, accept copies of independently published books, and avid readers write blogs dedicated to book reviews.

Send your book to reviewers who are interested in your genre. One of my clients wrote a book on parenting based on her twenty-five years as a marriage and family therapist and received an outstanding review from Dr. Dorothy Firman, co-author of *Chicken Soup for the Mother and Daughter Soul* and *Chicken Soup for the Father and Son Soul.*[13] Contact a magazine whose topic relates to the subject of your book; for example, if your book is about caring for dogs, send an ARC to a columnist at *Your Dog, Bark* or *Dog World*. Send a copy to a veterinarian who provides a newsletter to a large following through his website, and ask him to post a review. Contact experts in your field or your local newspaper's book or lifestyle columnists.

If you would like an interested colleague to review your book but he doesn't have time to read it from cover to cover, he might still be able to read an excerpt and compose a short review or endorsement. Take the time to prepare an attractive package for him, including a print-out of the front and back cover, title page, copyright page, table of contents, About the Author and the first three chapters. Add a blank page or two titled "Notes." To show your appreciation, send him the ARC or a copy of the final printed book or e-book.

A significant benefit of ARCs is that they give you the chance to perfect your book before the final print run. Reviewers often provide helpful feedback and note typos. They are aware that the review copy is not the final version and that even the cover could change. Make all the necessary adjustments to the interior or cover before sending the files for full production.

Tips for sending out review copies

- Your book designer can create a proper ARC cover for your book, and an editor can help with your cover letter.
- Print softcover books and plan your list of reviewers carefully to avoid overspending.
- Sending a PDF to avoid the expense of printing and mailing can have negative consequences. A PDF can easily be passed on

by email and displayed on any computer or device. Moreover, a PDF could find its way to a cavalier website based in Romania and turn into a free download; from there, free downloads could spiral out of control.

- There is no need to pay for a review. Most legitimate, highly respected reviewers read books and write about them without monetary compensation from authors and publishers.
- Many bloggers review books if they receive a free copy. Write to those who show an interest in your genre before mailing them a book.
- Refrain from asking an immediate family member or a child to write a review. Dissuade friends from posting the same review on multiple blogs and forums. Contributors to your book should not write a review; people will deem them partial because they have a financial interest in the book's success. Contrary to creating effective widespread publicity, these kinds of reviews tend to have a negative effect on prospective buyers.

Packaging is critical

John Kramer says, "Packaging is important. An instant judgment on your book is based on the packaging."[14] Packaging is how you present your book to reviewers, magazines, newspapers, distributors, booksellers and readers. Entice the receiver. Make him take notice.

📖 TALE:
>   One client wrote a book with a candy theme from be-ginning to end. He sent reviewers a handful of candies in small gift bags along with the ARC and cover letter, all attractively assembled and packaged.

When you send your book out for review, the package should be appealing and eye-catching.

Bad reviews

It can happen. If your book receives a negative review, take note of it and move on without responding. If the good reviews far outnumber the occasional negative comments, be grateful. When many people read a book, someone is bound to have a complaint. Look at the comment as an instrument of healthy controversy and discussion.

If your book receives many negative reviews, you may not have done due diligence to produce a quality product. Withdraw your book from publication, make all the revisions it needs and publish it with a new title, new cover and new ISBN.

More reviews

Continue to collect reviews after your book is published. You may find them on booksellers' websites, in blog comments or on social media websites.

What You Can Do Offline and Online

Offline publicity consists of activities done in person, on the telephone or by mail. Online marketing and networking take place through the Internet.

Offline and online publicity frequently overlap. Networking that starts through the Internet can lead to offline meetings and vice versa. For example, you might meet a radio show host through LinkedIn, correspond through email and meet in the studio for an interview. At a library reading, you might meet someone with a blog for writers who invites you to participate as his or her guest.

In this section, promotional activities are broadly organized into these two categories.

What You Can Do Offline

Your logo and your brand

Be sure that you have a professionally designed logo for your publishing company and all your promotional materials. The logo is the hub of your brand. It will influence the design of your website, business cards and promotional materials so they have the consistent look of your brand. This, in turn, will ensure that you avoid a rough or confusing presentation. Your brand visually identifies you and your product, like a thread that runs throughout your entire public profile and all your products and publicity campaigns.

Keep your logo simple so it looks good whether it's large or small enough to go at the bottom of your book's spine. Getting your logo designed does not have to be expensive, but it should be done by a professional. Avoid using icons and symbols that already available on the Internet. If the symbol is already used extensively, it won't present your unique product. Choose colors that represent your business identity, but note that it's the shape of and words in a logo that are critical. You can change the colors on different occasions. Be sure to get several file formats of your finished logo from your designer, including a vector graphic (with the extension AI or EPS), a JPEG and a TIFF.

Local media (newspaper, radio and television)

Members of the local media like to support local artists and writers, so take your book to your community. Explore book clubs, newspapers, the radio and television stations. Contact columnists and hosts who interview authors and send them a copy of your book. Check their websites, because some have guidelines or a form for authors to submit a request. Prepare your pitch before you contact them; tell them why your book would be of interest to their audiences.

Once the interview is scheduled, ask your host for a list of questions so you can make the session as worthwhile as possible for the audience. Practice answering the questions aloud, bearing in mind the length of the interview. Write down the key points and express them near the start, because the session will be over before you know it.

During the interview, stay relaxed, confident and friendly. Make sure your book title is mentioned at the start and end of your appearance, as well as where it is available. Request a copy of the recording to post on your website, and inquire whether the station or newspaper would place a link on their website to yours.

📖 TALE:

> One of my clients writes novels that take place partly in the Pacific Northwest, on Bainbridge Island near Seattle. Boats, kayaks and the local scenery are important in the lives of the characters and the development of the story. Local readers enjoy the book, but they are also proud of it and of the author. The real life setting even inspires tourists to visit the area. One reader's review said, "The descriptions of the places in the Pacific Northwest make me want to jump on a plane."[15]

Independent bookstores

Local independent bookstores can be great friends of independent publishers. Visit with a few copies of your book and see if they are willing to stock it. Independent bookstores often have websites, and if they list your book online, it may improve your book's ratings in the search engines.

Bookstore and library events

Contact bookstores and libraries to schedule readings and book signings. Well-organized events benefit the hosts by drawing people in, while generating interest in your publication. Extend your reach as far as possible—locally, regionally, nationally and internationally.

In a store, the venue for your reading or book signing should be inviting. Visit a few days in advance to check the area. Try to sit near the front of the store, where passers-by can see that an event is taking place. If the store can't provide a suitable table, bring your own, along with a, appropriate table cloth. Practice signing your name with the date on plain paper before the event, and decide whether you will write any additional words. Choose where on the title page or first page you are going to sign. Sometimes authors offer cookies, cupcakes or canapés to their visitors. Advance preparation will make the event go smoothly and pleasurably.

At the event, use a quality pen with permanent ink. Some customers may ask you to write their name (i.e., "To Carletta"). Hand them a notepad and a regular pen to print the name so that you spell it correctly. If you make an error, give the person a fresh book. Place your business card inside every copy.

Optionally, offer a custom bookmark (or another promotional gift) with each signed copy. Your book title, author's name and website should be clearly visible on the gift, along with a QR code if there is room. (See page 44 and 97 for information about QR codes.)

If you are inclined and the bookstore agrees, jazz up the event. Organize a contest. The winner gets a free extra copy of your book and a hat, mug or T-shirt decorated with a picture of your book cover and website address. To conduct the contest, prepare an attractive sign and a large piggy-bank-style transparent jar. Hand each customer a form on which he can write his name, phone number and email address before folding the paper and dropping it through the slot in the jar. (Make sure you have a privacy notice on the form saying you will never share the participant's contact information with anyone.) Announce the winner a week later and send the person his or her gifts by courier.

At a library reading, set up a table with a supply of books that people can purchase at the end of the event. Ask a friend or family member to sit beside the table throughout the reading so that you are free to engage with your attendees. Use any of the bookstore event suggestions above if the librarian finds them suitable.

School visits for children's books

If your book is for children, contact school principals or librarians to schedule your event. Make the presentation fun, interesting and educational. Be sure to send the children home with a small gift and a flier to show their parents so they can purchase your book. To get fresh inspiration for your event, research what different children's authors have done at school presentations by visiting their websites.

Book fairs

Throughout the year, book fairs are held in different cities around the world. All the major publishers and industry leaders attend the large international fairs, such as Book Expo America (BEA) and the Frankfurt Book Fair. Participants showcase new titles and services and discuss business.

Small publishers and self-publishers sometimes ask me whether they would benefit by displaying their books at BEA. I generally reply that if they are in the area, they should attend as a visitor: walk the aisles, browse the displays, talk to people and find out where the small presses exhibit to see if it would be worthwhile to invest in a renting a booth another year.

Usually, the large established companies that attend every year secure the best locations at a major fair. Novice entrepreneurs find the event overwhelming, and if they rent their own booth, it is expensive and located in an area that gets less traffic. Since a variety of titles is likely to attract more visitors than a single book, small and self-publishers often join together to rent a booth and share the expenses and benefits. Some writers' groups and publishers associations, such as the Association of Publishers for Special Sales (APSS, at spanpro.org) and Small Publishers, Artists and Writers Network (SPAWN, at spawn.org) provide this service for their members.

Business cards

Your business card is an essential tool that you can hand out liberally. When you network, you will likely receive as many cards from others as you give away. File those contacts for future reference. The business cards you receive may be even more valuable to you than those you hand out, because you will be able to contact the people you have met if a great opportunity arises or an ingenious networking idea occurs to you.

Carry a supply of cards to give out when you attend an event, and include them in every mailing. Distribute them

- at book fairs
- at writers' meetings
- at radio or television interviews

- in bookstores
- at library events
- to customers
- to educators
- with review packages sent to magazines, newspapers and independent reviewers
- to friends and family
- to colleagues

A business card should display your name, contact information, logo, book title and website, as well as a web page address where your book is available (such as your website or another online bookseller, or both). Have a full-color image of the cover on one side. If there is room, include a tag line or QR code. Print on both sides for maximum use of the real estate—but don't sacrifice visual appeal with crowded information! The card should be attractive at a glance.

QR code

QR stands for "quick response." The very name implies that the code will lead to an immediate benefit. Print a QR code whenever possible on your promotional materials, including bookmarks, posters, signs, fliers, sell sheets, business cards and brochures. A QR code stores and digitally presents various kinds of data; for a publisher, a website address and phone number are the most useful. When the image is scanned with a smartphone, a browser opens and the web page where your book is available displays immediately. Ask your book designer for more information about QR codes.

QR codes can also be printed on the back cover of your book or on an interior page. A QR Code looks like this:

☞ TIP:

> Bring a friend to every live presentation, whether it is at a bookstore, library, school or other venue. Ask that person to videotape your presentation. Make sure the microphone is pinned to your clothing to ensure that the sound quality is good, even if you walk around while speaking. Later, edit the recording as needed and post it online, either to showcase your ability and expertise or as a unique product.

What You Can Do Online

Press release

A press release is one of many ways to announce your book. Use it to generate interest through newspapers, radio, television and online media outlets, as well as targeted parties who are interested in your genre. Ideally, the press release will result in the various genres wanting to do a story on your book or you, the author. A press release, written in a standard format that journalists are accustomed to, should not be confused with an advertisement. Before you write a release, it's best to study a few samples online. These can be found at PRWeb.com and PRNewswire.com.

A press release should fit on one letter-size page and convey straight-to-the-point information about your book without graphics or colors. Put the most important information at the start so it reaches those who only read the first paragraph. The essentials:

- **top right:** your full contact information: name, address, phone, email address, website, and where the book can be purchased
- **top left or center in capital letters:** FOR IMMEDIATE RELEASE
- **center headline:** an interesting, newsworthy headline in bold capital letters
- **first paragraph:** the most important newsworthy information about your book
- **second or third paragraph:** more interesting information about your book
- **font:** Times New Roman or Courier, 12 point, black

If your budget allows, hire a professional. Many press release writers also distribute them to targeted audiences. They continually update their databases and can therefore assemble a long, targeted list of contacts who are interested in just about any subject.

A press release is part of every media kit. If you have a website, create a digital version that is available for downloading.

The template below is provided to help you write your own press release. Replace the words in square brackets with the information that pertains to your book.

[Contact information of
publishing company or individual]

[Publisher and/or Author] Announces the Release of
[Genre] Book
[Title of Book]

FOR IMMEDIATE RELEASE

[City, State] — [Publisher and/or Author] are/is proud to offer the [latest, debut, other adjective.] work from [Author's name], [Title of Book], available in bookstores everywhere on [date].

[Book title] is an/a [compelling story, informative guide] about/focused on [basic themes of book / subject matter covered].

[Further synopsis of book and/or details about the author that help to make the case that bookstores will want to buy copies of this because their customers won't be able to resist it].

[Quotes from author, and/or reviewers].

[Your Company Info]

Website

A website is like your own online magazine or catalogue, through which you can tell the world about your book, yourself and your events. You can post news, reviews and short excerpts from your book. Post articles on your subject with relevant information. Make your website inspiring, informative and friendly. Make sure it reflects you and your professional identity—your brand.

Obtain your own domain name from a venue such as GoDaddy.com, Hostgator.com or Namecheap.com. Not only do these providers' prices and options change regularly, but each of them offers different kinds of additional services, so shop around. Choose a domain name that reflects your company, your brand and your book. Ask your webmaster for help if you are not sure about which technical features you need.

If you are building a website for the first time, start with three pages.

- **home/landing page:** Post a good picture of your book with a catchy headline, an enticing description and excerpts from one or two impressive reviews. If your title has won awards, splash them right on the home page. Put your logo at the top of the page and repeat it on every page.
- **about the author:** Include a photo and a bio that describes your experience, your credentials and any information that will advance your book.
- **contact:** This should enable interested parties to reach you easily by email and regular mail. If you want to keep your privacy protected and you don't want to post your contact information online, ask your webmaster to create a web page with a form that has a field for the visitor's name, email address and message. If your contact information is at your home, consider getting a post office box for book-related mail and a dedicated phone number for your office. That way, when buyers call, they won't accidentally speak to your children.
- **additional pages:** These might offer resources, a blog, an interview, your news or products related to your book.

Make it easy for visitors to buy your book by putting a **call to action** on every page. Your call to action includes words and graphics that say or mean, "Buy now!" There should be a clickable link that adds your book to their shopping cart or takes them to a purchasing page.

Even if you sell your book from your website, post links that go directly to your book page on major booksellers' websites. Online shoppers tend to be most comfortable buying from venues they know and trust. Giants like Amazon like to discount their prices to be the lowest on the Web, so avoid undercutting them.

To create your website, either use a template-based format like WordPress or hire a website designer who uses software like Dreamweaver. The advantage of a template-based site is that you can update it yourself whenever you want to post something new or make a change. A website designer can make you a unique design and maintain the site for you.

Post scheduled book signings, presentations, online workshops, webinars, radio interviews and television appearances to showcase your activities as an author.

You may wish to offer products that correspond to your book, such as CDs and workbooks. Sometimes a percentage of the proceeds goes to a charity. Children's book authors sell caps or T-shirts with pictures of the characters in the story.

📖 TALE:

A client of mine wrote and published an acclaimed, award-winning book dedicated to saving the environment by teaching people how to make informed and humane food decisions. The author contributes all proceeds from her book sales to SaveNature.org and Edible EdVentures.[16]

Another client publishes picture books that help children learn American Sign Language (for the deaf). A percentage of sales from the book and related products goes to a local children's support organization.[17]

☞ TIP:

Buy your own domain name so you retain full control of your content, regardless of what happens to your hosting service. Your domain name should relate to your book title or the services and products you provide.

☞ TIP:

> Make sure you have a call to action on every page. Give your visitors "buy now" options that link to your book's page on the websites of major booksellers.

☞ TIP:

> If you have more than one business, don't mix unrelated content on the same website. Offer your visitors the kind of quality content they expect, and try to exceed their expectations.

Online sellers

Some of the best-known online booksellers in the US are Amazon and Barnes & Noble, Indigo-Chapters and Abe Books in Canada, and Waterstone's and WH Smith in the UK. Sell softcover, hardcover and e-book editions of your book from these sites to maximize your sales. Customers trust them, and they get an enormous amount of traffic, so they are your best online vendors. Enable the Search Inside feature so that people can browse through your book as they would in a regular store. Add other online sellers, depending on whether or not you find the setup fees and plans reasonable. You might not get many additional sales, but more avenues mean more prospects, and even a few extra sales each week can add up.

On Amazon, create an Author's Page and ask people you know who have purchased your book to write a positive review.

☞ TIP:

> Another option is to engage the services of a **distributor**. If you use print-on-demand, Lightning Source has a wide-reaching distribution program that makes your book available on websites around the world. You won't have to set up your own account everywhere—you can do so only on the websites that don't partner with your distributor. Read about distribution and fulfillment in Chapter 8, "Printing Books and Fulfilling Orders."

Book trailers and YouTube

Book trailers are powerful marketing tools if they are made and used cleverly. Your book trailer should look professional and succeed in creating interest in your book. Keep it very simple or put in a mix of elements. Possibilities abound:

- narration about the book
- the author speaking about how he wrote the book
- music
- text on slides
- pictures on slides
- actors representing the characters in a novel
- a single simple setting
- a creative mélange of backgrounds and effects
- a call to action: "Click here to buy this book"

A direct call to action at the end is vital: "Click here to buy this book," or something similar, should link to a purchase page.

Either produce your book trailer yourself or hire an expert. If you do it yourself, use good recording equipment and quality images. A tinny sound, bad lighting or blurry slides might make the viewer think your book is just as faulty as your film and cost you sales.

Some clever book trailers show the author presenting his book in an unadorned setting. At the end, the video should show the website addresses where the book is available with a picture of the book cover. Though this kind of trailer seems simple to make, it has to be done well to be effective. Book trailers for fiction may have music, readable text, narration and performing actors who convey the flavor of the story. To get ideas for your book trailer, watch a selection of them on YouTube. You will be inspired by how diverse they can be.

Upload your book trailer to various websites, especially YouTube and your own, using well-chosen keywords. Be savvy—make several trailers of different lengths that showcase your book in various ways, each with a different soundtrack. Post them all online to increase exposure. (You can upload several trailers to a website made for video uploads, but put only one on your own site.)

☛ TIP:

> Using a service like Animoto.com can make the video-creation process easy. It offers a variety a themes, audio soundtracks and payment plans. Have fun playing with the features and make a test version first. Then polish and produce your book trailers to post online.

☛ TIP:

> Using video-editing tools like Camtasia from TechSmith. com, you can make a professional book trailer. This kind of software has a steeper learning curve than a template-based service, but TechSmith provides many online tutorials for those who want to learn.

Email signatures

Your email signature serves the same purpose as your business card. Include your name, book title and website. You could even add a pithy excerpt from a positive, influential review and a link to your book page on a major bookseller's website.

Business cards and email signatures work for you. You just have to use them!

Build your platform online: blogs and virtual tours

A virtual book tour entails visiting different websites and bloggers' sites and posting on those sites in various ways—by keying in a comment, sending the site owner a typed interview or arranging with the owner to be interviewed on a podcast, which will be streamed live or recorded to be played later.

A virtual book tour is a tool for promoting your book online. Both fiction and nonfiction authors create online tours to get their books read, reviewed and exposed. Choose sites that already show an interest in books in your genre or in your general topic. Bloggers post frequently and may have a large or small "fan base"—a list of people who regularly visit to see what is new on the site. Those fans are likely to be interested in your book.

After researching online and making your list of book bloggers, contact those who have a large following and are therefore best positioned to help you. Tell them about your book and say you are starting an online tour. Offer them a copy and request that they review it. Ask if they would be willing to host you on their blog or to talk about your book, and arrange a specific date for your contribution.

Bloggers benefit by hosting authors whose books will interest their followers and help attract new members. Authors benefit by gaining publicity for their book.

What does a virtual book tour involve? A blogger might invite you to do any of the following:

- be a guest writer for the blog
- answer questions in a written interview: the blogger sends you questions, you type the answers and he posts the interview
- be interviewed on a podcast (an online radio show)
- participate in a book giveaway
- contribute to a contest that generates interest in your book

On the virtual tour, you might also do the following:

- write reviews for other books
- participate in social networking events
- tweet on Twitter and post on Facebook

All this is designed to gain publicity—to give you and your book a recognizable public profile, which, in turn, should generate sales.

A virtual tour takes time and energy. It needs to be well-planned to be effective. If the research and planning seem too time-consuming, hire an expert. Internet publicity experts have lists of bloggers categorized by genre, and they keep their eyes open for new bloggers all the time. Publicists organize virtual tours and generate other types of publicity, too.

Do your research, make inquiries and use the services that work best for you and your budget.

Do virtual book tours work? As with all forms of publicity and promotion, for some authors, they are highly successful, and for others, they are less effective.

A virtual book tour can be done as part of the launch of a new book. It can also work any time after the book is published to put your book back in front of the public eye and boost sales.

Social media websites

Facebook, Twitter, YouTube, Pinterest and Google Plus are the some of the most popular social media networks, but there are scores of others, too, such as StumbleUpon, MySpace, Meetup and Digg. Do you need them? Some say that if your audience is on a social network, you should be, too—and since so many people are involved in social networking, it's fair to assume that at least some of your audience uses these sites.

Social media websites can be time-consuming—too time-consuming for some people. If you are new to them, start with Facebook, Twitter and LinkedIn, and make a schedule to develop your presence. For example, spend an hour on Monday, Wednesday and Saturday each week. Set a time limit so you only do what is worthwhile without getting carried away. In this way, you can build your online presence steadily and systematically.

Alternatively, hire an Internet publicist to kick off your social media campaign and develop it for two or three months; then continue on your own. You could engage a virtual assistant to post regularly on your behalf, but you will have to spend time training him or her.

Below is a list of the five most popular social media sites. Familiarize yourself with each site and with what members expect before you post. Start with one and add others when you are ready. Statistics about the different social media websites can help you plan your campaign. To know more, visit Ignite Social Media at ignitesocialmedia.com.

On **Facebook**, you can create a fan page so that people interested in your topic see your news. You can also create a closed Facebook group if you have a membership of people interested in your topic or you offer a course related to your book; there, members can interact and support each other. Try to get **likes** for your pages, without dwelling too much on the numbers. Likes will grow organically if you keep up your campaign.

Tweeting on **Twitter** is an easy way to get news out in small doses. Since the maximum number of characters in a tweet is 140, think of posting once or twice every day, or a few times a week. If you are tweeting a URL, shorten it at tinyurl.com so you have enough characters left to complete your tweet. Learn how to use **hashtags**[18] to organize posts about your book. A Twitter hashtag is a keyword phrase, written without spaces and preceded by a hash sign (#). For example, the hashtag for this book is **#publishandsucceed**. Choose a unique, short hashtag for your book and add it to all your promotional materials. Put it on the back cover of your book, along with your website address, QR code and other contact information. Make it part of your email signature.

YouTube is enormously popular, and video is a powerful means of increasing interest in your book. Read the section of this chapter about book trailers. (See page 103.) You can make several trailers, each focusing on a different aspect of your book and on you as a writer or expert. Optimize your keywords for each video you post online. Don't forget to include the call to action and the URL where your book can be purchased.

Pinterest is primarily for sharing photos. Make a page for your book and **pin** (Pinterest jargon for "post") pictures of the cover and an infographic about your book. If you display at a book fair, pin a few enticing photos of your booth. If you have a library or bookstore event, post photos. Make a collage. The possibilities are endless. Display images that support your marketing campaign, rather than personal or family photos. You don't have to pin a photo of your dog if you don't want to.

Google Plus is newer than the other sites mentioned, but some analysts advise that if you join early, you might be noticed more readily because of the moderate competition. The main features are social **circles**—people can join each other's circles, Google's version of a network or personal group—and **hangouts**, where people can meet online in real time.

LinkedIn is last in this list because it is a **professional network**, rather than a social network. On LinkedIn, professionals connect and interact through groups and connections. Complete your professional profile, add connections and update news about your book so that people who work in fields related to yours can find you.

There are a few guidelines to remember when using social networking to publicize your book:

- Provide valuable content and appreciate others. Shameless self-promotion is frowned upon.
- If you find social networking overwhelming, establish a solid foundation on the site of your choice, rather than dabbling in all of them.

- Try to post content that creates an emotional response. Tell a true story that is relevant to your book and your audience. Use humor skillfully.
- Participate regularly, but not obsessively. Post thoughts, perceptions, suggestions, excerpts, experiences—be creative. The post does not have to be long, but it should be worthwhile for the reader.
- Keep your target audience and media influencers in mind when posting. Talk to them.

For increasing your book's visibility and sales, some popular social media strategies will not be worth your time, such as the following:

- trying to get thousands of followers on Twitter: most will not read your tweets.
- sending your newsletter to everyone who comments on one of your posts: this could annoy people who didn't sign up and induce them to report your newsletter as spam.
- fretting about social media ratings. Generally, they have nothing to do with your target audience. Just use social media websites the way you use other tools: respect other users and contribute quality tweets, posts and comments. This will increase your visibility and exposure.

Book contests and awards

Winning an award in a respected contest can give your book sales a big boost. Contests are conducted throughout the year, around the world. There are national and regional contests, as well as contests conducted by institutions, associations, newspapers and magazines. Registration for major contests is usually open for books by authors from different places, but some are region- or country-specific.

Awards can accelerate your marketing campaign. They impress readers because they say someone in the publishing industry read your book, enjoyed it and judged it more valuable than others in the same category. The more highly respected the contest, the more powerful the award.

Contests are not just for "best book of the year." They have categories, beginning with fiction, nonfiction and poetry, which are subdivided into various genres and target age groups. In most contests, a book can place first, second or third (or win gold, silver or bronze) in its category. An honorable mention or being on the list of finalists also carries weight and is something to be proud of. Your book could win an award for cover design, interior book design, illustrations or e-book cover design. If your book wins an award, use it to publicize your book.

Consider your book's strengths and enter it in whatever categories you think it can succeed. A title can usually be entered in more than one category, so if you think you have an excellent young adult novel with a spectacular cover, enter it in both categories. Whether your book is about saving the environment, car mechanics or flying kites, you will find suitable categories. Several contests are only for books that target the large Christian market, others are for poetry and some are just for e-books.

Certain awards include a cash prize. That can be an exciting bonus, but it should not be the main incentive. If your book wins any reputable a contest, you will have cause to celebrate.

Publicize your award! Post its emblem on your website, add it to your email signature and print it on your business card and bookmarks. If you print using POD, revise your book cover to include the emblem on the front cover. If you have printed stock, adhere a quality, lightweight sticker.

Most competitions have an entry fee. Fees cover the costs of holding the competition and publicizing it. Research the various awards and choose the ones that you think you have the best chance of winning.

An award adds value to your book. Use it to its fullest potential.

☞ TIP:

> Only enter contests whose awards would increase your book sales and publicity. A contest should have a history, be respected in the publishing industry and have a limited number of winners and honorable mentions. (Some "contests" give an award to almost every entry, and that renders the awards insignificant at best.)

☛ TIP:

> It doesn't have to be a Bloomsbury or New York Times National Book Award to be worthwhile. Research the contests you are interested in, compare them and then decide which ones to enter.

Small publishers' associations

Several small writers and publishers' associations offer benefits to their members, such as discounts on marketing campaigns, group displays at book fairs, publicity strategy advice, publishing news and events and forums where you can converse with other members and share problems and solutions. Research these organizations online, compare membership fees and benefits and then decide which is right for you. Below are is a short list of some excellent organizations:

- Association of Publishers for Special Sales (APSS), spanpro.org
- Small Publishers, Artists and Writers Network (SPAWN), spawn.org
- Independent Book Publishers Association (IBPA), ibpa-online.org
- Christian Small Publishers Association (CSPA), christianpublishers.net
- Society of Children's Book Writers and Illustrators (SCBWI), scbwi.org

A Few More Things You Can Do Online and Offline

Below are some suggestions that require time but little or no cost to implement:

- Plan your book launch around a related holiday
- Link your book to a charity. Conduct events that coincide with the charity's calendar and publicize the fact that you are giving a percentage of proceeds from sales to the charity.

- If your book is nonfiction, offer a free seminar on the subject at a bookstore. This enables people to learn about the topic and meet the author while providing your book with exposure. Have an assistant record your presentation with quality recording equipment, and if you have a Q&A session at the end, ask him or her to hold the microphone for each questioner. Test the sound a few hours ahead of time or the day before in case you have to make technical adjustments. Edit the recording later and post it online. Give other presentations at bookstores in different locales.
- Create free events like the one described above and sell your books there.
- Record all the data from every presentation until you have enough sales and information to entice larger enterprises to carry your book and let you present there.
- If you have more than one title, bundle your books and offer them at a discount on your website. Add a promotional gift if you like.
- On your website, offer a discount code for the purchase of three books. Call it a "gift code." Print bookmarks with the information and gift code, and place them inside books you ship yourself.
- Build a fan base through your blog, Facebook, Twitter, Flickr, Pinterest and other networking sites. If you are a children's writer, create a page on JacketFlap.com.
- Write articles with valuable content on the subject of your book and send them to targeted magazines, websites or ezine sites. Always include your bio and a link to where your book can be purchased.
- Place your book in non-bookstore shops; for example, pet stores for books about animals, gardening stores for books about flowers and shrubs or kitchen stores for cookbooks. Try to place your books in your favorite local gift shops and stores.

Keep your expenses within your budget

Some of the ideas mentioned in this chapter can be implemented very cost-effectively, or even for free. Others require that you spend money or hire a professional. Define your budget and do what you can do comfortably. Make an engaging book trailer, for example, but spend less than 10% of your marketing budget on it.

Keep your promotion and marketing costs down and your activity healthy. By creating and following a pre-defined strategy, with funds allocated for each element of your marketing plan, you will be able to keep publicizing your book for a long time.

Final Words

This chapter presents a range of ideas you can use to market and publicize your book. Once you start, your creative channels will open and new possibilities will appear on their own.

Engage in various forms of book promotion. Marketing and publicity require energy, time and dedication. It is important to continue and not to give up a few months after publication. Do something regularly that contributes to your book publicity, sales or expansion of your professional network.

Often, the best promoter is the author. If your book isn't promoted, no one will know about it. If people don't know about it, they won't be able to buy it.

Today, the opportunities for publishing and book promotion are changing constantly. Be on the lookout for new ideas to publicize your book. The possibilities are endless.

Publish and Succeed!

Where Preparation Meets Opportunity

I HOPE THAT AFTER READING THIS BOOK, you have gained the knowledge and confidence you need to publish your book.

Effort, time and passion are needed for book production. It starts with inspiration, moves on to writing and editing and then to perfecting your creation for your readers. You may have some of the skills needed, but for a quality publication, it's best to hire professionals to execute the steps with which you are unfamiliar or inexperienced. If you try to do everything yourself, you are likely to spend a considerable amount of time creating an amateur product instead of a high quality book produced by your own skilled team.

With this in mind, I suggest that you hire an editor and book designer and engage someone to produce your e-book. Create an attractive, effective website, starting with just a few pages and adding others over time only as needed. If you do this, your book will shine and your entire project will be in gear to impress. Moreover, during the production process, you will have time for your family, your friends, a walk in the countryside, a concert, a party—all the other enjoyable things in life.

When the time comes for post-production marketing and promoting, you will be ready to embark on the last phase. Continue to adopt new means to promote your book. When you have done a presentation in your local bookstores, move to other counties or regions, or contact libraries. Post news about your engagements on the social and professional networks—both information ahead of time about when and where the event will be held and a follow-up description with pictures. Continue to use both online and offline techniques to market your book. Above all, keep enjoying the process.

Having prepared a quality publication, you will be ready to meet any opportunity that arises. If you are invited to give a presentation on your subject, you will be able to display your book with pride, and without feeling apologetic because you fell short anywhere. Newfangled possibilities will spring up—be sure to take advantage of them. Create new situations—people will be interested, so don't deny them or yourself the pleasure. All your preparation, following the steps outlined in this book, will enable you to take new steps, because you and your book will be ready to succeed.

Final words

Persevere! Success is born of a quality product, a catchy presentation, hope, tenacity, networking with people who can help your book succeed and connecting with the most important people of all—your readers.

"Success is where preparation and opportunity meet,"[19] said race car driver Robert William "Bobby" Unser. These words ring true for the successful writer and publisher.

The word "success" means different things to different people. Whatever your meaning may be, success is the reason you are writing and publishing. Others should get the benefit of your experience, your creativity and your knowledge through your book, while you have the rewarding sense of satisfaction and accomplishment.

Part 3
The Author

People should *appreciate* your book and say,
"Other people would enjoy this book, too!"

Q & A
The Inside Scoop on Editing

Kelley Hunsicker: What does it take to become a professional editor?

Jill Ronsley: An editor needs impeccable grammar, punctuation, spelling, an extensive vocabulary, a firm grasp of syntax, or sentence structure, and a good sense of language.

Her job is to return a polished manuscript to the author. A professional editor should have complete familiarity with at least one of the major editing style books, such as *The Chicago Manual of Style* and preferably with more than one style. With this kind of solid basis, she can adjust to the personal style of most writers or the in-house style of a publishing house or magazine.

Specialized editors work with medical, scientific or technical writing. They need a thorough knowledge of the discipline to ensure that terms are used correctly and clearly. Some editors do fact-checking to verify that a research project has no inaccuracies.

Kelley: How many years have you been a professional editor?

Jill: I have been working as an editor for over twenty years, both in-house and freelance. Over the past few years, I have worked as a freelancer.

Kelley: What does a professional editing service do?

Jill: An individual or a business can hire an editor through a professional editing service to edit any sort of manuscript, such as a nonfiction book or novel, a short story, a magazine article, a cookbook, a dissertation, a work in translation, a manual, an interview, letters, reports, speeches, brochures, website content and so on.

Before a writer submits a manuscript to a prospective publisher, he or she may hire an editor to polish his or her work, as well as the cover letter. Sometimes, before submitting an assignment to his boss, someone hires an editor to refine the language and ensure that it is error-free. Writers hire editors to review their manuscripts and rework them before submitting to publishers.

Kelley: Why is using a professional editing service beneficial to children's writers?

Jill: For the same reasons that it helps all writers. Whether the manuscript is written for adults or children, the grammar, flow of language, punctuation, choice of vocabulary, spelling and so on should be accurate and appropriate. These details immensely affect the telling of a story. To the reader or publisher, errors in the text are like coffee stains on a shirt to the eye. On the other hand, a polished manuscript has a flow and clarity that makes it a joy to read.

Kelley: How can a writer know whether an editor will do a good job on his or her work?

Jill: An experienced editor can provide references. She may provide a sample edit to a prospective client so the writer can see the quality of work she provides.

Kelley: How long does it take to have a manuscript edited?

Jill: That depends on two things: the length of the manuscript and the kind of corrections required. An editor might complete a letter or brochure in an hour or less. A complex work, such as a novel, cookbook or manual, requires more time. If a client has a deadline, I always let him or her know whether I will be able to meet it.

There are two basic categories of copyediting. Standard editing involves checking for grammatical, spelling and punctuation errors. This can be done quite quickly. Substantive editing involves reorganizing sections of a manuscript and rewriting or consolidating the text, in addition to the regular work done on a standard edit.

A writer might have brilliant, creative ideas or something very worthwhile to say, but he or she may lack the complete writing and editing skills needed to turn out an error-free book. The editor ensures that in the final stage of the creative writing process, the text is excellent.

Kelley: What kind of changes do you make to manuscripts?

Jill: When I work on a text, I eliminate wordiness and refine the sentence structure. Frequent mistakes that detract from the quality of a story or book are dangling participles, overuse of modifiers, repetition that causes the reader to lose interest in the story, excessive use of passive language, faulty sentence structure and illogical organization of the thoughts that the writer is trying to communicate. Sometimes, the idea a writer wants to convey is perfectly clear to him, but he doesn't realize that the writing isn't communicating effectively to the reader. Of course, grammatical, punctuation and spelling errors must be amended. An editor reads with a fine-tooth comb.

Kelley: Do you edit magazine articles, too? If so, how long does it take, and what is the cost?

Jill: Of course! Magazine articles are a significant category, one that I particularly enjoy. Editing all sorts of texts is rewarding—long or short, fiction or nonfiction, stories for children, youths and adults. Rates are determined by the length of a manuscript and the time required to finish a job, as well as the kind of editing required, standard or substantive. This applies to magazine articles, books, cookbooks, short stories, brochures, website content and so on.

Kelley: If editors at publishing houses request changes for a manuscript, why is a professional editing service an asset to a writer?

Jill: A manuscript worked on by a professional editor will be error-free. When the acquisitions editor at a publishing house reads an error-free manuscript, she will immediately sense that the writer is a professional. She will not have to look past the flaws to find the story. The acquisitions editor may still make recommendations for changes if she is considering accepting the manuscript—after all, she is an editor, and she will always have her own suggestions!—but these will certainly be fewer and less complex than they would have been if a manuscript editor had not already made revisions.

Kelley: Is there anything else you'd like to add?

Jill: Yes! I love my work, and I enjoy working on all sorts of manuscripts. Everyone has something interesting to write. It may be educational, humorous, sad, compelling, technical, poetic, enlightening or something completely different. Rendering the written word into clear and sometimes beautiful language is my passion. That is why I enjoy working with writers of all genres, from all different backgrounds.

And there you have it! The "Inside Scoop" on editors and the services they provide!

Kelley Hunsicker specializes in writing nonfiction for children, but she also writes general fiction and nonfiction. Her articles and books have been published by several magazines and publishing houses. She was the founder and first president of BOOST4Writers. This interview was first published in The Blue Review, *March 2004. It is reprinted with permission.*

About the Author

WITH 15 YEARS' EXPERIENCE, JILL RONSLEY is a distinguished figure in the publishing industry today. Over her career, she has assisted not only established mainstream publishers and authors but also independent publishers, small presses and budding authors in a variety of capacities, from writer and editor to book designer, publishing consultant and e-book producer.

She counts *New York Times* bestselling authors, Canadian literary publishers and British educational publishers among her international list of clients, and she has contributed to many award-winning books in different genres. She won the Best Book Editor 2005 award from the Editors and Preditors Readers Poll and has served as a judge in several writing competitions. In her magazine career, she has been a copy editor for Canada's leading glossy lifestyle magazine, *La Dolce Vita Magazine,* and *City Life,* and for three years was editor-in-chief of the *Blue Review,* formerly a monthly e-zine for children's writers available by subscription, for which she also wrote two columns.

Founder of Blue Star Press Inc and its divisions, Sun Editing & Book Design (www.suneditwrite.com) and Publish & Succeed (www.publishandsucceed.com), Jill has also established herself as a renowned designer for a wide variety of books, from self-help, business and scholarly texts to novels, children's books, poetry and film scripts.

A member of the Bay Area Editors Forum, the Canadian Authors Association and Adobe InDesign and Photoshop User Groups, she has published numerous articles on editing, book design, writing and publishing and has presented at writers' conferences, events and workshops in the US, Canada and the UK. She has been a guest speaker at St. James School in England and her media contributions include guest interview on "The Writing Show."

A lifetime student of the art of language, Jill earned a BA at McGill University. She studied fine art at McGill and the Montreal Museum of Fine Arts, and she received a diploma in languages and literature from Vanier College, where she studied English literature, French, German and Italian. She studied Classical Western and Eastern philosophy, Hindi and Sanskrit at McGill and French at the University of Grenoble.

Jill has frequently travelled in Europe and Asia. Having grown up in Montreal, she has a passion for international culture, art, history and music, as well as meditation, yoga and healthy living.

Work with the Author

If you have written a book, Jill would be happy to hear from you. She offers a free 15-MINUTE PHONE CALL to discuss the best options for your title. Send her an email to set up an appointment.

If you would like a DONE-FOR-YOU BOOK for your business or an ULTIMATE CALLING CARD, contact her to learn about the BUSINESS PACKAGES she offers.

www.publishandsucceed.com | www.suneditwrite.com
jill@publishandsucceed.com | jill@suneditwrite.com

Visit www.publishandsucceed.com for
more information, news and promotions.

Interior Book Page Illustrations

Page 38

1. Sarah Itzhaki, *Wizarday: When Our Stuff Went Away*. Bethel: Toys'NTayls, 2010.

2. S. L. Whyte, *The Stelladaur Series:* Book 1—*Finding Tir Na Nog*. Seattle: Fireglass Publishing, 2012.

3. L. M. Ruttkay, *RV the Racer Aardvark*. San Marcos: Fishgate Media, Inc, 2010.

4. Marc Franco, *The Kringle Chronicles Series:* Book 1—*Catching Santa*. Winter Garden: Pants on Fire Press, 2011.

Page 39

5. Mike Gabor, *Training the Average Person to Be an Extraordinary Athlete*. Zephyr Cove: Mountain Paddler, 2012.

6. Heidi Schultz, Martin P. Block, Don E. Schultz, *Understanding China's Digital Generation: A marketer's guide to understanding young Chinese consumers*. Worthington: Prosper Publishing, 2013.

7. Ilene Val-Essen, Ph.D., *Bring Out the Best in Your Child and Your Self: Creating a Family Based on Mutual Respect*. Culver City: Quality Parenting, 2010.

8. Julie Ann Martin, *Travel-Ready Packing: Pack Light, Dress Right—Anytime, Anywhere*. Los Angeles: Argo & Cole, 2009.

End Notes

1. Dan Poynter, "Publishing Poynters," Para Publishing LLC. July 2013, accessed August 2013, http://parapub.com/files/newsletter/PP-EZINE%20JULY%201,%202013.docx.pdf,

2. Gary Price, "New Statistics from Bowker: Self-Publishing Sees Triple-Digit Growth in Just Five Years," October 24, 2012, accessed August 2013, http://www.infodocket.com/2012/10/24/new-statistics-from-bowker-self-publishing-sees-triple-digit-growth-in-just-five-years/.

3. Nick Morgan, "Thinking of Self-Publishing Your Book in 2013? Here's What You Need to Know," January 8, 2013, accessed August 2013, http://www.forbes.com/sites/nickmorgan/2013/01/08/thinking-of-self-publishing-your-book-in-2013-heres-what-you-need-to-know/

4. Darren Simon, email message to author, January 30, 2011.

5. James Felici, *The Complete Manual of Typography: A Guide to setting Perfect Type*. Berkeley: Peachpit Press, 2003.

6. Matt Mayerchak, Principal, Mayerchak + Company. Printed with permission, 2013.

7. John Kramer, "Book Promotion Tips: Book Promotion: The 10 Things You Can Do to Promote Your Books." (http://www.bookmarket.com/bookpromotion.htm)

8. Marianne Bickle, *The Changing American Consumer*. Worthington: Prosper Business Development Corporation, 2011.

9. Gary Chapman and Rick Osborne, *A Perfect Pet for Peyton*. Chicago: Northfield Publishing, 2012.

10. "Digital Book World, "Ebook Best-Sellers $3.00 to $7.99, Week Ending 6-9-13," June 11, 2013, accessed August 2013, http://www.digitalbookworld.com/2013/ebook-best-sellers-3-00-to-7-99-week-ending-6-9-13/.

11. Jeremy Greenfield, "Avg. Best-Seller Price Continues to Tick up as Big Publishers Score Hits," June 18, 2013, accessed August 2013, http://www.digitalbookworld.com/2013/avg-best-seller-price-continues-to-tick-up-as-big-publishers-score-hits/?et_mid=623972&rid=26910752.

12. Gregory Ciotti, "The New 4 P's of Marketing," January 23, 2013, accessed August 2013, https://www.helpscout.net/blog/new-4ps-of-marketing/.

13. Ilene Val-Essen, Ph. D., *Bring Out the Best in Your Child and Your Self: Creating a Child Based on Mutual Respect.* Culver City: Quality Parenting, 2010.

14. John Kramer, "Book Promotion Tips: Book Promotion: The 10 Things You Can Do to Promote Your Books," accessed August 2013, http://www.bookmarket.com/bookpromotion.htm.

15. See S. L. Whyte, *The Stelladaur Series:* Book 1—*Finding Tir Na Nog* and subsequent books in the series. Seattle: Fireglass Publishing, 2012.

16. See Linda Riebel. *The Green Foodprint.* Lafayette: Print and Pixel Books, 2011.

17. See Kentrell Martin, *Shelly Series: Book 1—Shelly's Outdoor Adventure. Book 2—Shelly Goes to the Zoo.* Land O' Lakes: Shelly's Adventures LLC, 2013.

18. Magdalena Georgieva, "How to Use Hashtags on Twitter: A Simple Guide for Marketers," accessed August 2013, http://blog.hubspot.com/blog/tabid/6307/bid/32497/How-to-Use-Hashtags-on-Twitter-A-Simple-Guide-for-Marketers.aspx.

19. Bobby Unser, accessed August 2013, http://www.brainyquote.com/quotes/quotes/b/bobbyunser126431.html.

5682681R00082

Made in the USA
San Bernardino, CA
16 November 2013